To Mame,

With very best wishes,

Ruth.

Making the Best of It
Building on the Bonds Between Parents and Adult Children

M. RUTH WHYBROW, M.S.W.

D0112222

Old City Books
Copyright 2011

DEDICATION

To my parents
George and Doris Steele

And my daughters
Kate and Helen

And grandchildren
Chase, Willoughby, Gavin, Willa and Wren

Acknowledgments

Over the past decades as a psychotherapist, I have met and talked with many older people and their children, some of them together, some separately. Most frequently they visited me in my office, while others attended groups or workshops that I led. All shared the hopes and fears, joys and concerns of their lives as they impacted or were impacted by their families. I have learned so much from them, and thank them all.

Beyond my professional work I have talked with countless other people about their relationships with their parents or adult children. I found that this subject of great interest to me was also a topic that most people in their middle and older years wanted to talk about. Though too many to mention, these friends, colleagues, family and, also strangers have taught me a great deal and I appreciate their insights and openness.

For help in the production of this book, I would like to thank Kate Siepmann for her design skills, Dorian Yates for sharing her publishing experience, and Sandra Smith-Ordway whose eagle eye produced a finer polish. This book would not exist without them.

CONTENTS

Introduction

Families have always fascinated me. So, many years ago, when I began to take a special interest in working with older people as a psychotherapist, discussions about their relationships with their adult children were inevitable. Many of my older clients wanted to discuss their worries and difficulties with their families. Meanwhile younger clients sometimes wondered how better to understand and improve the interaction with their parents. It was the concerns of both groups that encouraged me to embark on this book.

I have seen many people—friends as well as clients—struggling with, and even endangering, one of the most important connections in their lives. The damage is caused rarely by neglect, but rather by well-meaning efforts on the part of each to help or change the other—efforts that sometimes backfire, leaving both parties feeling hurt, angry and puzzled. For me, too, this is a subject close to my heart. I have mother who is 97-years-old, and daughters who are well into adulthood with homes and families of their own.

Of all relationships, the one between parent and child is the most compelling. For children, it is the most influential for parents, the most fulfilling and most worrying; and, for many years, the most consuming in both time and energy. Whether close or distant, a source of pleasure or pain, this bond remains an important one in which indifference is rare. It is long lasting—more so now than at any period in human history. For the first time, children can expect their parents to reach advanced old age, while parents often have children who have retired from work, and have grandchildren who are raising the fourth generation. Throughout these many decades we are called upon to adapt to innumerable new situations. Whether expected or unseen, welcomed or dreaded, direct or indirect, change impacts us all. Therein lie our challenges and the subject of this book.

Over the years we parents have helped our children grow from helpless infants to competence and then to independence. We have loosened control, either voluntarily or because our children pushed us to do so. Now independent, they have skills and knowledge different from and often beyond ours. They have people more central to them than we are and thus create lives away from us. We are changing too. We have relationships, interests and jobs that take more of our attention than our children. Contact with each other is more a matter of choice than it has ever been, depending on proximity and affection rather than on need. Our families expand to include in-laws and grandchildren. Then, as we age and begin to fail, the balance shifts again with our children taking on some responsibilities for us. All this may or may not fit our expectations. Real life is not predictable, however, and certainly no fairy tale. For all of us there are demands we did not foresee. Nor are we always sure how to meet them.

By the time our children reach adulthood our authority over them has dwindled, but our influence has not. Herein lies a question that all parents have to face. How do we let go of the habit, and perhaps the wish, to control and effectively use our influence for the good? The watchfulness and authority that were once part of our relationship with our children are out of place. Now our interactions are built on the feelings we have toward each other.

Like my clients, I ask myself how to nurture these relationships. How to be supportive of my daughters without interfering, how to convey trust and confidence when I have doubts about their choices, how to be helpful without eroding their sense of competence? As a daughter, I along with my siblings, discuss with each other and our mother how best to help her maintain her precious independence. For myself, I debate how to balance my wish to be emotionally close and to be a resource for them all with my other responsibilities and interests.

In this book I will try to indicate how you can influence the quality of your interaction with your family and ride some of the bumps inevitable in any relationship. It is not totally up to you of course. Each of you has your own set of life events—many of them difficult and even heartbreaking—but even under circumstances that look bleak, try to keep your hope alive. Positive change may be small and appear more slowly than you would like but appear it will.

I come to this topic with some opinions that I have formed over the many years I have been a therapist. Before I go further, let me clarify my point of view. First, I assume that your children are important to you, and that you are to them. You want a relationship that is warm and mutually supportive. Angry, estranged and disappointed though you may be at times, you are never uncaring. This goes for both parents and children. Second, I will repeat my belief that you can affect your relationship for the better and that is never too late to try. Third, you must relate to your children differently as they age. I am stating the obvious but, if you are honest, you know that sometimes you think and act as if you can live your grown children's lives better than they can. You want everything to be right for them so it seems imperative to step in and provide the answers. Your instincts may be misguided, however—as may be your answers. You need to let go your inclination to control, whether you do it by advice, bribery, or criticism. You sometimes disagree with them, and say so, but that can be done with thoughtfulness and without judgment. Your adult children are for the most part able to make their own decisions and find their own way to carry them out. Even if you could do that for them, it would dilute their sense of achievement. Your support, love and interest are as vital as they have ever been. So important are they that is where to put your energy, thereby helping your children grow and your relationships flourish.

Over the course of this book we will be considering the common dilemmas that affect most families with adult children. After the first chapter that sketches the context in which both parents and their children have grown up and now live, each of the subsequent chapters focuses on a particular issue of relevance to us all. At the end of each chapter is a list of the main points. My hope is that this book will throw light on some of your concerns and troubles and that the suggestions will be of practical use to you.

The information I present comes from several sources. Primarily it is drawn from my clinical work over many years with a variety of clients whom I have seen as individuals, as couples or in groups. I have learned a great deal from these people. In addition I have had many conversations with friends, family and colleagues about relationships with grown children or parents, and have listened with awe to their hopes, disappointments, struggles and victories.

Our relationship with each family member is not exactly like any other. And our spouse's relationship with each will be different as well. The interaction of our personalities, our history, our needs is unique. That does not mean, however, that we do not have much in common with other parents and adult children. We have similar questions and concerns. From my own experience and from the stories told to me I have distilled some insights that I hope will be helpful. I believe that with good intent, with some personal awareness and with love, we can all—parents and children—do much to create the kind of relationship that nurtures and enriches each of us.

Setting the Scene

The relationship between us and our adult children typically lasts decades longer than their childhood but receives relatively little attention in the literature on human development. Those of us whose children are grown know that parenting has not come to an end, but it has certainly changed. Now, our interactions are between adults who care about each other but can exert no authority. Despite the many shifts in our lives we know that our bond will remain important to us all for as long as we exist, and we fervently hope it will be a loving one.

No two connections look alike. From the self-contained nuclear family to large extended networks, from children who stay close to home to those who spread their wings, from cultures where most relatives live together to those where large distances separate kin from kin, the variety is infinite. But emotionally there are many similarities. Our American culture with its emphasis on the individual puts little social pressure on adult children to be close to their parents, geographically or emotionally. Rather, the push in early adulthood is towards separation and autonomy. Despite our cultural bias, however, the vast majority of us do choose to stay in touch and to care about each other.

By the time our children reach early adulthood they probably no longer need us in order to survive. The contact between us is now a choice: one in which children usually have the greater power. Their time and energy goes more into building new relationships, homes and financial security than into thinking about us. This is a period for us to let go. Much used to be written about the empty nest stage and the loss that parents, especially mothers, experienced, but in today's world parents seem too busy and content to be distressed for long. Letting our children go, as we must, entails some adjustment, but we would not choose to have it otherwise. Watching our children set out on their own road and knowing that we have done our job, we typically have a pleasant sense of accomplishment.

The gains that come at this stage of life more than balance the losses. Most of us enjoy our post-parenting years with their greater personal choice and freedom. We may have more in common with our children now that they are holding a job and making their own home. Conversing with them about their interests and activities may be a new pleasure. Then the family will expand as in-laws and grandchildren are added to the mix.

As with everything in life there is no guarantee of happiness. As we and our children grow and change we have work to do if our relationship is to be a fulfilling one. I say "we" because for the most part it is the parents who make most of the effort. We are the ones who must relinquish control, accept the partners our children bring into the family and watch them all make decisions we sometimes think unwise. For us our relationship with our children is so significant that we will do almost anything to avoid endangering it. Not that our children do not care. Of course they do—a great deal. Like us, they want a respectful, loving relationship, but not at the cost of losing their autonomy.

So we are both, parents and children, beginning a new stage of our lives. As we progress we will doubtless head in different directions but the threads remain connected. The many challenges we meet are the subjects of the chapters that follow. Here, in order to outline the phases that almost universally occur in families, I want to provide a context for our interactions with our children.

A DIFFERENT TIME

Our children are living in a very different world from the one in which we reached adulthood. Mothers are almost universally employed outside the home, struggling to meet the demands that jobs and children bring. Fathers remain preoccupied by their work but are more hands-on parents than their fathers were. Children are born into a world more dangerous, polluted and challenging than in our day. Divorce, blended and stepfamilies add to this complex environment.

In this ever-changing world perhaps it is not surprising that children take longer than we did to settle into their lives. They may try several jobs before deciding on a career, and many relationships, some live-in, before deciding on marriage, which often comes later than in our generation. They may return home to their parents during transition times. We are sometimes amazed when we watch our mid-20-year-olds and recall that at their age we had babies, our own home and were financially independent. Meanwhile they often take time off from college or work to "find themselves" or to travel before they make any long term decisions. They seem to want more materially and live less frugally, whereas we spent, and probably still do, only within our means. Socially, Americans are much more mobile than when we were young. Since grown children often live far from their families of origin, contact between the generations may be quite difficult and costly. Gone are the weekly Sunday meals when the whole family gathered. Times are different indeed.

Our life experience may be of interest to our children—or maybe not—but it is of limited use. Remembering the chronic fatigue and ceaseless demands that came with my own small children, I could appreciate what my daughters were going through when my grandchildren were little. But with many of my daughters' concerns I have little direct experience. I can share their fears about the temptations of drugs and alcohol, the prevalence of sexual abuse, and empathize with the difficulties of working outside their home and making time to watch a child's soccer game, but I have never lived in their world. As I buckle my grandchildren in and out of seat belts and bicycle helmets I am grateful that I raised my children in a more innocent and simpler time.

As I look at young people I see them more willing than we were to protest and to try to change what they dislike about their relationships or their lives. They seem to have higher expectations than we had. People of our generation, especially women, expected to make the best with what they were handed, including their marriages. Men were invariably the breadwinners, women the primary parents and homemakers. Now both partners typically earn money, men are active parents and together they put a high premium on love and emotional support. Unfortunately, high expectations often lead to personal discontent and an increase in the divorce rate.

The ways our children seek help have also changed. Rather than turn to the church or pastor for guidance, for instance, they are more inclined to consult mental health professionals. What they regard as a resource, our generation often looks at with suspicion. Born at a time when people were less open about their feelings especially with strangers, we may have little experience with self-examination, and less patience with it. Often I have heard people say about their adult children, "They are so self indulgent. If I hear, 'I need to take care of myself,' again, I'll scream."

Despite their misgivings many older clients have come to see me because they wanted to please a child, usually a daughter, who has encouraged them to see a therapist. The daughter sees her parent struggling with grief, or other emotional difficulties and suggests a service that she herself has probably found useful. In my experience these clients intended to come once in order to satisfy their child, but to their surprise find the conversations helpful. Many of them engage in therapy with an openness that would surprise their children.

In a myriad ways our world is changing at an increasingly rapid rate and as we age we find it difficult to keep up. Sometimes we are not interested in doing so. Most older people are resilient, however, and willing to try new services, such as mental health, and technologies, such as the internet, and adopt whatever they find useful. As in all generations, though, innovation may cause apprehension in the elderly as they foresee dangerous influences to be faced by future children. But it is not helpful to give advice in a world that is so different from the one we knew. Nor is it useful to spend too much time bemoaning changes we do not like but that are here to stay. What we can do is focus on what has always been important—fostering a warm, respectful and interested relationship with the young people we love, and keep an open mind.

NEW LANDMARKS

During the extensive period of our relationship with our adult children much happens to us all. As in every interaction whatever affects one person also affects the other. Our children create homes away from us, we retire, new members join the family as children marry and have children of their own, and we age and probably need some care before we die. Much more occurs, of course, but these are the almost predictable landmarks in a life.

For parents, our home empties gradually through high school and college. By the time our children reach their early 20s, we have become accustomed to their long absences and their relative self-sufficiency, and have begun to look forward to their independence being complete. No more dirty laundry, no tuition bills, no more children coming home in the early hours of the morning. We can hardly wait. We anticipate more freedom, and the lessened sense of responsibility and financial burden. Used to worrying about where our children are and what they are doing, we find it easier to relax in our ignorance. "What I don't know doesn't bother me," is a truism that brings relief.

Watching our children grow into adults brings much satisfaction most of the time. We take pleasure in their increasing competence, their skills and knowledge that are different from ours. Two of my happiest memories come from this period when my daughters were in their early 20s. Each of them took me on an outing that she knew I would enjoy. One took me on a canoeing expedition. From the moment that she met me at the airport, she was the expert. I had never been to Minnesota, never canoed, found my way through lakes and portages, or camped on remote islands. My other daughter took me rock climbing, something I had always wanted to try. Alone at the foot of a huge rock, she took the end of my rope in case I fell, and called up instructions and encouragement. I was so proud of both girls, their competence and professionalism. Both events were highlights in my life as a parent and marked a shift in how I viewed them.

Not everything is happy and easy of course. We continue to worry at times, we disapprove, or we may even feel used or neglected. It was easier, we sometimes think, when the kids were young and we had some control. Some parents complain that their adult children never visit and their phone calls are infrequent and often short. "I've learned to dread the words, 'I have to go.' It's the sign that my time is up." Other parents find that being too important has its downside. "I wish our nest were empty. He's come home again."

As our children begin to create families of their own the situation alters again. The arrival of a grandchild is a major event in any family. Parents and children have something

huge in common—someone whom they both love uncon-
ditionally. There is a new focus of attention that involves
pride, love and endless talk.

Many people find that there is a favorable shift in family relationships when a child is born. Our children seem to
have suddenly become responsible and secure in their independence. Difficulties left over from adolescence and
early adulthood are put to rest. Mothers and daughters often
renew a close bond, while fathers, as grandparents, delight
their children by showing more affection and joy than they
did as parents. Conversations and visits become longer and
more frequent.

Most parents adore being grandparents and are in turn
loved by their grandchildren. But that is probably all that
grandparents have in common. Grandparents come in
many different models. Some like nothing so much as being
with their grandchildren, whereas others want a break from
the caregiving that they feel they have been doing all their
lives. Others enjoy playing with and reading to young children but are unwilling to have the responsibility of caring
for them alone. Older grandparents love to hold babies but
find toddlers too exhausting to be with for long. Grandparents who live far away or are occupied with jobs and activities may have to struggle to find time to be with their
grandchildren, supplementing their visits with letters and
phone calls.

Our children are as gratified to watch us love their
youngsters as we are to love them. But our pleasure in them
does not necessarily mean that we are ready to drop everything in order to see them. The truth is that our children

and grandchildren are not our only priority and occasionally we want to say "no" to a request for us to care for them. Unless you are always pleased to be with your grandchildren, you are probably wise to make sure that your children know you have a busy life and that your arms cannot always be open.

Another significant landmark of mature adulthood is retirement and one that most of us anticipate with pleasure. We may be disoriented for a short while as we learn to deal with the looser structure of our day, create a different social life and find new fulfilling activities. In general, women adjust to retirement quite easily, probably because the routine of housekeeping is a constant, retired or not. Women are also more likely to have a social network that is not built around a job. For men their work largely defines who they are and how they spend most of their waking hours, so the adjustment may take a little longer. Couples may find more time together to be a plus, or a minus. However fond a couple, the statement "I married him for better or worse but not for lunch," remains true for many. Single people of both sexes sometimes face a greater challenge if work filled most of their social needs. On the other hand they may be experienced at finding new friends and interests.

Before long most people settle into this new stage of their lives, and find much to enjoy. You may embrace the opportunities to travel, do those chores and projects you have been thinking about for so long, take on some volunteer work and spend more time with the family. Your children may begin to make comments about how rarely you are home and how lovely it must be to have relaxed vacations. Now they are the ones who are more confined than you. And that continues as the grandchildren grow. By their teens they are usually so busy with sports and friends that if you want to see them or your children you have to do the traveling.

Meanwhile we are changing as we age. Eventually we become less active, stay at home more and find that our families have become even more important to us. Indeed it is their families that give most elderly people some sense of place and purpose. As they watch their grandchildren and great grandchildren grow they have a feeling of continuity that gives meaning to their lives. "It is so nice that she wanted to know," said my mother after her granddaughter asked about her first job away from home at the age of 14.

Many old people become increasingly introspective, thinking about the past and wondering whether their life has been, and still is, worthwhile. For them this question may be difficult to answer. "Am I of use to anyone now?" "Do I matter?" The generation that is old now has tended to assess its value in terms of service to others. "I'm happy if I can help someone." For my mother at 97 it is very important to her that she can still cook for her family. We had a conversation recently about whether she could still make the Christmas cakes that she always bakes for each part of her family. Shopping, mixing and lifting are all a problem. Knowing what her answer would be, I nevertheless suggested she end the tradition. "But I don't want to give it up," she said, "and I do think everyone enjoys them."

For most of our lives we have given more help to our children than they have to us, but at some time that will almost certainly change. No longer is it common for parents to move in with their children, nor do most parents want to do so, but for most infirm parents their children do become an important resource, physically and especially emotionally. And children spend more time concerned about their parents and trying to help them manage. Should parents have to be cared for in a nursing home—something that everyone tries to avoid but it is not always possible to do so—children are usually still much involved, providing the kind of love and attention that only they can give. There are many aspects of life at this stage that make life difficult for everyone but few parents fail to feel grateful for the help and care that their children give, and children appreciate being able to return some of the love and support that they have received.

Letting Go

> *"You are the bows from which your children as*
> *living arrows are sent forth."*

Like many young mothers, I was much taken by this beautiful line from Kahlil Gibran's *The Prophet*. Less elegantly, we say, "You have to let them go."

We all nod in agreement, but what exactly does that mean? Sending our children forth was a process that began at birth. When they were young, we needed to guide them in most aspects of their lives and when they strayed, draw them back to safety. But before long we allowed them to make some choices, encouraged them to do things for themselves, and even to make mistakes. The boundaries we imposed on our children evolved with their maturity. It was a learning experience for all of us.

As bows, we are vital, providing the strength and resilience necessary for our children's flight. Just as arrows in flight are affected by many factors—their individual properties, the wind and terrain—so our children are subject to many influences. We are one of many. Once the arrow is launched, however, the bow that was indispensable has no more control. Its work is done.

For many parents, letting go of control is exceedingly difficult to do. We have protected our children for so long that we may continue to try to assume responsibility for their lives, even when such attention is no longer appropriate. For years we have arranged holidays, taken trips, arranged activities, all with our children's wellbeing in mind. Mothers in particular tend to feel that the happiness of everyone in the family depends on their efforts. "All I want is for my children to be happy" we say, and mean it. As children mature, however, that goal becomes so elusive and personal that we cannot reach it for them. When our children are ready to let go of us, their destination is no longer in our hands.

Letting go may be the preeminent challenge of parenthood. The first time our children crossed the road or walked to a friend's house alone, we tried to watch without being noticed, feigning an ease we did not feel. Later, they made their first trip alone and we waited anxiously for the phone call announcing that they had arrived. In due time they went off to college and marriage. We watched their progress with a mixture of pride at their achievements and sadness as they moved away from us. Our job has been to help them become competent, self-sufficient beings for whom we are no longer essential.

What does this letting go or sending forth mean for our relationship with this adult who is also our child? Surely it is not the same as turning away?

For parents and our children, the relationship between us is one of the most vital in our lives. It evolves into a bond between equals—equals who care deeply about each other but also respect each other's decisions and opinions even when we disagree. Paradoxically, it is only by letting go of the control we once had that we remain connected. The time for authority is past. Love and support, however, are always and forever, important.

Given all the opportunities we have had over the years for practicing letting go, why does it remain difficult? We give out more advice than our children appreciate, we try to pass on the wisdom we consider we have gathered over the years, and we assume that our experience is helpful to them. For their part, our children may take our advice too easily just because it comes from us; more likely, they reject it for the same reason. These habits formed over a long period are hard to break. If our thoughts are to have any chance of being useful or appreciated we need to take care about when and how we deliver them.

Our children have reached the stage when they are responsible for their own lives. If we appear critical or authoritative, we are sending a message that we do not trust them to manage, and they are likely to feel diminished and inadequate. They are exquisitely attuned to our thoughts, even if unspoken. My children use a somewhat bored "Yes, Mum," to indicate that they know what I am about to say, and that I don't need to. So what are the signals that our opinion or advice is not welcome at this moment? If your children sound annoyed, defensive or uninterested, it is time to back off. That you consider your advice invaluable is irrelevant.

I asked one of my daughters how she felt about advice from me. "Oh, that's fine," she said, "I can take it or leave it." I was relieved. In my experience, however, if parents give unsought advice on sensitive topics, their children often hear criticism. We need to be aware of our tone and be ready to retreat.

Over the years I have met with many parents and their adult children for whom the tension has mounted to the level where they seek professional help. One woman and her son had come to such an impasse that any time spent together was a cold war. She disapproved of his wife, and the way they raised their children, and could not refrain from dropping unsubtle hints about changes they should make. She already knew her interventions were resented, but like most us in a difficult situation, she responded in the only way she knew how. Her son did the same, increasing his pleas for her to conceal her disapproval, even though he too knew his requests would be ignored. They were stuck. Meanwhile his wife and children made every excuse to avoid her visits.

Despite this family's discomfort they had not quite given up on each other. One thing I learned as a therapist is that even small changes are often significant. I was not at all sure that therapy would help but in fact they did make some changes. The mother was able to be less obvious about her negative feelings, and the son and his wife showed their appreciation of her efforts. I am sure that neither ceased to think that the other was misguided, but they were able to move away from an unpleasant confrontation. Visits though probably not fully relaxed, were at least taking place.

Some families have inbuilt strengths that help them deal with inevitable tensions. A sense of humor is one of these strengths. I admire families where parents and children can be outspoken and teasingly affectionate at the same time. The balm of humor is that messages can be clear, but feelings not hurt. A friend was recounting a conversation with her son after she had given him some advice about his children. "You know, Mum, we're a sovereign nation here." "You're right", she replied, "but that doesn't stop us having diplomatic relations." They both laughed.

Many of us do not have that tradition of banter, and may find it difficult to deal with even minor disagreements. We take our opinions and those of others too seriously.

Sometimes the disagreement is too significant for anyone to find place for levity. A couple described one of the most painful times of their lives: in her early 20s, their daughter announced that she needed not to see her parents for a while. They could write, and she would too, but they were not to see or talk to each other. Of course the couple was devastated. They were unbearably hurt, worried and angry. What had they done to deserve this? Where had they gone wrong? In response to their questions and pleas, their daughter was not forthcoming, saying something about finding her own way. They knew that she had some difficulties socially, but why could she not talk to them as she used to? They felt they had no option but to attempt to understand her, wish her well, and write regularly. After about 18 months their daughter reappeared, seeming more confident and comfortable with herself. In retrospect the couple agreed that, as a family, they were all strong-minded. Perhaps there was not enough space for this particular child to chart a different course. At the very least they came to understand why she had taken some action, but were still not convinced that it had to be so drastic.

To respect their daughter's wishes was, I'm sure, one of the hardest things this couple ever had to do. They told me they had no choice, but in fact they had. They might have criticized her, pleaded with her, or blamed her for their own distress. Instead, they decided to act as if they trusted her to do what she felt she needed to do.

"Acting as if" is an essential tool at times. I have talked about respecting our children's ability to live their own lives, but sometimes parents find it impossible to have that trust. "But look at the decisions he's made!" "Her history with relationships is awful." Our concerns may be totally justified but we need to be careful about when and how we voice them. Expressing our own thoughts to our children, without judgment, briefly and once, may serve some purpose, but try to refrain from voicing your doubts unless asked.

At a meditation retreat I attended, one of the participants asked about detachment, or letting go. Over her years of meditation practice she thought she had made progress in this area, with one important exception: her children. She still worried about possible problems, imagined tragedies, and handed out advice that was neither solicited nor appreciated. Was there something different about parent and child relationships? The leaders looked at each other, laughed, and said that as parents of a teenage girl, they did think there was a special challenge. It often seems impossible to be tolerant and calm where our affections run strongest.

Another client told me of her concerns about her 28-year-old daughter. "I know she's irritated when I hand out my advice and opinions, but I can't seem to stop. Last night I called to wish her happy birthday and what did I do, despite my best intentions, but launch into advice mode again. Immediately she said 'I have to go now' and she did."

This woman has an important advantage in her quest for an easier relationship with her daughter: she has self-awareness. Her intent was to be more attentive, and to listen with an open mind. And she recognized that she had failed to do so—this time.

Though far from simple, letting go of our need to guide and control is worth the effort. Indeed, we have no choice. Our children have the same drive to stand on their own feet—just as we did, and do—and will do it with or without our encouragement. It is far better to watch lovingly as they exercise their right and responsibility to live their own lives and make their own mistakes than to alienate them with our advice. It is for us to show interest, be willing to try to understand and, above all, to be an anchor in hard times. It is a critical, but not controlling, role.

WHEN CHILDREN DON'T LET GO

For some of us, the issue is not so much our letting go as our children failing to do so. "If only we were lucky enough to have an empty nest," complained one father. As young people today tend to marry later and divorce more often, there has been a growing trend towards staying in, or returning to, their parents' household.

Most children who go back to the fold as adults, do so temporarily. They are motivated to leave again under their own power and do so as soon as they are able. Others stay because they and their parents find it mutually convenient and agreeable to share chores and expenses. Still other children have a disability and continue to need the help that their parents can provide.

It is not that unusual for an adult child, in some way disenchanted with life, to return home, to be supported by his parents, and stay on for years. One couple's son who dropped out of college returned home with no plan in mind. At first his parents assumed that he would find work, but nothing seemed to suit him. Perhaps the right job would turn up, they thought, therapy might help, or he needs time to mature. The situation stretched into years, and hopes of his independence became more and more remote. They were all stuck.

Having an adult child at home, who for no apparent reason seems unmotivated to make a life of her own, is one of those situations about which advice abounds and solutions are elusive. Whether training babies to sleep through the night, persuading children to dress instead of playing on school mornings, or dealing with a young adult who wants to live at home, other parent's problems seem much easier to solve than our own—until we meet our own.

Many children take it for granted that they will be welcomed home. Each of us handles the request differently. Here are some useful guidelines. One: try to hold back your unconditional assent by taking their request seriously as one that deserves, and requires, thought and discussion. Two: be completely honest with yourself about any hesitations or reservations you may have. Though awkward, talk openly with your child about your feelings. Three: ask questions, listen and encourage them to voice their concerns. If it still feels a viable idea, fix a trial period and agree on a date when you will all evaluate how the arrangement is working for each of you. Do not rush the discussion. All of you may need time to consider what you have learned before making a decision.

Your child is not stepping back into the same house he or she left. You are different and so is your child. When your children leave home, you embark on a new stage of your lives. You may enjoy the peace and privacy, and the ability to make plans without having to consider anyone except yourselves. Be mindful that if it was an adjustment when the children left home, it will be a greater one if they return.

As I write, I'm well aware that I would not find it easy to place any condition on my welcome if I were to receive such a request from either of my daughters. Intellectually, I know I do not have to say yes, but my heart equivocates. Does that mean that I welcome them with open arms, as if nothing would give me greater pleasure? I hope not. I would like us to be honest with each other, voicing our expectations and reservations so that we enter this new arrangement as well prepared as possible.

A friend described how he and his wife handled their daughter's request to come home for a while. She had been sick and wanted space and comfort to recover and think about a job change. What better place than home? They did have some questions, however. How long did she anticipate staying? How would she go about job hunting? What would she do with her time? Before long, she was waiting tables at the local restaurant, and within three months she moved to permanent work and her own apartment.

That family situation was easy to resolve largely because their daughter had no wish to remain attached to her parents; nor had they any desire for her to do so. Perhaps no discussion was necessary but at the very least, it signaled that her request was a special circumstance and merited serious attention. Their conversation probably prevented some of the ambiguities and tensions that are inevitable when adult children and parents live together again.

Some situations are not so easy to resolve. For the "stuck" couple that I mentioned earlier, it probably didn't occur to them at first that their son would not soon move on to create his own life apart from them. They never set any limits on his stay or behavior. As time went on, they found that it was too late to do so. Friends and family advised them to put him out—tough love—but this was not advice they could follow. We all want to do the right thing but sometimes it seems there is no such thing.

Family dynamics that are deeply entrenched are very difficult to change. Earlier on, this couple might have pushed their son toward some sort of independence, by insisting that he take a job whether he thought he would like it or not, and that he do certain chores at home. If they had had the resources, perhaps they could have rented a room for him, paying some advance rent, but no more. But by the time I met them, their will had dried up and his ability to care for himself had atrophied. I, honestly, had no solution to offer. The only course is to take mindful steps along the way to avoid the quagmire.

What about children who do not live at home but are still more financially and emotionally needy than you wish they were? A son asks regularly for help with his credit card debt. A daughter calls you frequently, and at length, to bemoan her lot in life, never saying anything positive or asking about you. In such cases you have developed the habit of obliging, regardless of its inconvenience to you. Again it takes resolve to break the habit. Before you take any action, however, ask yourself what you might lose if you no longer had this problem. It may seem a strange question but often we maintain a distasteful habit because it gives us something we do not want to lose. Are you afraid you will never hear from your son if you cut off the handouts? Do your daughter's outpourings really give meaning and interest to your life? Do you give them everything they ask for in an attempt to compensate for some perceived inadequacy on your part? We parents may so enjoy being needed, or be so afraid of losing our children's love that we are incapable of saying no. Unfortunately, this impulse may curtail their development and our own.

If you do decide to alter your response to your child, give some thought to when and to what you will say. Impulsiveness rarely works. Caught at an inconvenient or irritable moment, we can all lose our patience and with it, any chance of effectiveness. After all, we bear some responsibility for our child's dependency on us. We have allowed and perhaps encouraged it. It is only fair to give them some warning that their behavior is no longer acceptable. You might tell your son that you are ending the bailouts and give him a date to prepare for that. Perhaps tell your daughter that you have been thinking about your conversations, that you want to be supportive but would like to include other subjects when you talk. Take the initiative in changing the subject. If this does not work you might have to shorten the calls.

We all have different styles of parenting. Even in optimal circumstances, however, parenting is a challenge. On occasion, we may have concerns about some pattern of interaction with a particular child. Our feelings can guide us. Regularly occurring anger, resentment or distress are all serious danger signals. Stop there and reflect what is really going on between you.

WHY AREN'T THEY THE WAY I WANT THEM TO BE?

New and young parents are often admonished not to build expectations about their children—whether it is who they will resemble, what attributes they will have, even what gender they will be. The rationale is, I suppose, that parents might put undue pressure on their child to fulfill parental dreams. Before I was a mother, I remember thinking such advice was so self-evident that it was unnecessary. Of course, I thought, I would not push my interests on my children. I would have no problem recognizing that their talents and choices were not the same as mine. And it would be no problem when they chose friends that I disliked. It was not long before I realized how naive I was. Without recognizing it, I did expect them to be like me in many ways. I never doubted that they would enjoy the outdoors, like to read, even be good students. And in fact, we do share much, likes and dislikes, and therein rests much comfort and pleasure. We are, however, very different,

Raising a child whose differences from you are clear from the start may present some challenges. One mother of grown children recently said to me that raising her daughter was easy—"she seems to raise herself"—whereas her active, impulsive son was constantly surprising her. Often we react with delight to see interests and talents in our children that bear little resemblance to our own. We may enjoy their love of sport or their interest in machines because they are new arenas for us. I admire the spunkiness of one young granddaughter and the equanimity of the other. Neither characteristic is as marked in any other member of the family. If instead of interest in our differences, however, we react with intolerance we send a destructive message to the child we love. Perhaps a parent who has little spirit of adventure sees an active child as irresponsible or dangerously impulsive. If everyone in the family except one likes to read, that one may be labeled as disruptive and a nuisance. If we can see the individuality of each of our children, our love will be a source of strength to them and joy to us.

Of course, we have dreams for our children that go beyond temperament or interests. To feel good about themselves and their place in the world, to have a sense of fulfillment, to give and receive love, are all hopes we hold for them. To have wishes and hopes is natural. Problems arise if they become expectations. To our way of thinking perhaps our children can only be happy if they choose partners of the opposite gender, the same social and educational background, if they work at a job that fits the capabilities we think they have, and if they have children of their own. But these are only our notions of what will bring them happiness.

What makes us think our way of being and doing is the right or only way? Of course, we are products of our own childhoods and culture so it is our own experience that guides us. Born into a different world, however, our children are likely to face problems and possibilities that we could never have imagined. I remember how surprised my husband and I were when our daughter said she would like to take a year off college. Unaware at that time that such arrangements were quite common in this country, we had many doubts. Her reasons made good sense and of course she thrived and we learned something about keeping a more open mind.

Look at the social revolution that has occurred in the West in the last 40 years. With the prevalence of premarital sex, divorce, wider acceptance of homosexuality, and women working outside the home, our children mature in a very different climate. We can listen, perhaps guide, and certainly learn from them. At times, we look at the world through blinders, seeing only what we judge as right or wise. Our discussions would have more space for interest and respect if we were less invested in others agreeing with us. Perhaps we might not be totally right, or the others might at least have a point. We can be open to our children's views, and still preserve our own integrity.

WHY AREN'T THEY FRIENDS?

"I just wish they liked each other more," said a friend of her children. Like most people who are reaching old age, my friend was wondering if her children would look out for each other when she was gone. In most families the mother is the hub of gatherings and often the communication link between the various members. As siblings live far apart, divorce and remarry, and have little in common except parents and their childhoods there is certainly no guarantee that anyone will see the need for acting as the family link. Nevertheless many people do maintain meaningful connections with their siblings, connections that last until death.

Much as we want our children to be good friends, we can do little about it. We cannot make them love or even like each other. But there are some things we can refrain from doing. It is vital to stay out of the middle of your children's relationships with each other. If one complains about another, encourage her to speak to her siblings directly. Carrying messages from one child to another usually causes resentment.

Sibling rivalry is inevitable. My parents made considerable efforts to treat all their children alike but we did not always see it that way. My sisters and I were convinced that my brother was the favorite, my brother thinks that as the oldest I had preferential treatment, whereas I saw that my younger siblings were treated more leniently than I. Our feelings exist though not one of us can produce any evidence for them. Comparing old memories usually triggers laughter but, under certain circumstances, old rivalries are revived. Many people find family gatherings uncomfortable as feelings of annoyance, rejection and jealousy that they thought they had left behind long ago, come to the surface. "What is it about my parents' house that makes me act like a teenager?' asked one client.

The truth is that we do not treat all our children exactly the same. They are individuals with their own personalities and needs and, because we too are unique, our interactions are like no other. Your children may not complain directly that you prefer one sibling to another but there may be subtle or not-so-subtle hints. "You see a lot of her." "You seem closer to his children." The inference is clear. "You like my sibling and his children more than me or mine." For your part, you have good reasons for acting as you do— "She needs the help," or "They live nearby so it easy to see each other,"—but your explanations are unlikely to satisfy them. Attention, like money, often represents love, and our children, though grown, are sensitive to how much they receive compared with their siblings. When we sense that a child feels less loved we can take note and address it appropriately to their circumstances and personality.

When adult children do like each other we may not always react with delight. We may feel left out or even jealous as we see our children choosing to spend some time together without us. A client complained that her children had gone away for a weekend and she had not been invited. This was unusual because she saw a great deal of her children, but this was a hiking trip, something in which she could no longer participate. Though she knew the facts she still felt angry and bitter.

MONEY

Money is often a source of problems. When in short supply, it becomes a preoccupation for parents as they struggle to meet their family's needs. Ironically, money can create more awkward questions in affluent families. How much will the parents provide financial help for their children, and under what conditions? When or how is giving money constructive? When does it foster dependence or encourage a sense of entitlement?

Parents usually plan to treat their children fairly. But what is "fair?" Some parents give each of their children equal amounts of money, keeping a running account of incidental gifts and balancing accounts over the years. Others give according to need as they see it. Some would rather give than loan, or vice versa.

Money is a very powerful issue within families because of its symbolic power. It represents control, favoritism, love or guilt. We may be sure that we do not exert control over our children with our money but we probably do find it easier to meet a request that we approve of rather than one that appears frivolous. Helping out with education is more likely to appeal than funding a fancy car.

Each family and each situation is so different that it is impossible to make more than general suggestions. First of all, if you do not have discretionary income there is no money to lend or give; you have to take care of your household's needs first. However you and your spouse decide to handle your money, it is wise to share your philosophy with your children. If you give more to one than another, it is easier for your children if they learn about it from you. Though your reasons make perfect sense to you, the child who receives less will almost certainly feel less loved. Of course it is your money and your decision how you spend it, but if you can be open with your children the more likely you will avoid dissension. If you explain, for instance, that you are giving more to the one who needs it, your children may not agree with you but are not likely to feel unloved. If you want to attach conditions to your gift, be sure to talk clearly about them ahead of time. I remember one client who paid her daughter's fare home for Christmas, and was angry because her daughter spent more time with her friends than her mother. Both felt sore and badly treated.

Though most parents are reluctant to share their financial status with their children there comes a time when it might be helpful to give them a fuller picture. If your children ask you for money you cannot afford, it is in your interests to let them know that. They may think you are better off than you are. Conversely, they may think you have little money and anticipate that you might need their help. Again, better to let them know.

GUILT

Believing that it was up to us to shape our children's character is an awesome responsibility. No wonder the word "guilt" emerges so often in any discussion among parents. Is that painful feeling an inevitable part of parenthood? Perhaps. Certainly it is on occasion. We parents have made mistakes for which it is appropriate to feel guilty. We were short-tempered when our children did nothing to deserve it, or we may have been quick to chastise one child more often than the others. Guilt is an important sign that we have done something wrong, and we know it. With that information we can consider what to do. We might apologize, resolve not to behave in that way again, or seek help if our behavior is a chronic problem. Carrying guilt around, however, is almost never useful.

Much of the guilt people feel has no sound basis. Mothers in particular tend to attribute much that goes amiss in their children's lives to their faulty parenting.

They even feel guilty if they fail to be available or loving at all times, or even when a child is unhappy. This is inappropriate guilt. An adult child's divorce, drug habit, unemployment, or untidiness cannot be blamed on the action or inaction of their parents.

A major problem with inappropriate guilt is that it puts responsibility in the wrong place. Your child needs to learn and accept that the ownership for her behavior resides with her. For you to assume the blame will hinder her maturation and ability to be self-sufficient.

I think we often use "guilt" when "regret" is more accurate. Most of us ordinary human beings have many regrets. We certainly regret that our divorce gave our children distress. We are sad that the chronic illness of one child took much of our attention from the others. We may be sorry that we cannot meet our child's request to help with the grandchildren.

So we are not perfect. And we do not have to be. I have always been much comforted by a phrase coined by a British child psychiatrist, Dr. D.W. Winnicott. He wrote about a child needing a "good enough" mother. (If he were writing now instead of 50 years ago doubtless he would have replaced "mother" by "parent".) At some time, we have to accept that we parented as well as we were able and must let go of any expectation of perfection. Instead, let us try to appreciate what version of "good enough" we have been and our children are becoming.

POINTS TO CONSIDER

- Letting go of control is essential if our children are to mature into independent adults.

- Letting go does not mean that you no longer care. Our support and love remain as critical as ever.

- When children want to return home, you will all find it helpful to discuss how long they plan to stay, how they will contribute to the household and to set a date for evaluating the arrangement.

- Beware of expectations. Your children are individuals and need to make their own decisions, choose their own life style and their own partners.

- However much we wish it, we cannot make our children like each other. Acting as a go-between only makes matters more contentious.

- In families, money is more than cash. It represents love, control, favoritism, or guilt. You will probably have your own philosophy about whether or not you help your children financially, and how you do it.

- You can ease possible feelings of rejection and resentment if you make clear your thinking on the subject.

- Guilt is an over-used word in many parents' vocabulary. Of course apologies are called for when we hurt someone, but carrying guilty feelings around forever helps no one. A wise older woman once said, "Don't allow guilt house room."

- All parents make mistakes but, for the most part, we do the best we can with what we have and know at the time. Regret is usually more appropriate than guilt.

Communicating

This chapter focuses on a subject whose importance I stress time and time again because it plays an essential part in every other topic I address. What we convey to each other and how we do it affects every aspect of our being with others. We try to transmit what we think, what we feel, what we want and, by listening, we strive to understand the same of others. When effective, communication helps with almost all problems; when not effective, it makes most problems worse.

Human communication is a complicated business, made up of many different components. Verbal language is the one we are most conscious of, but tone of voice, timing and the way we use our bodies are other ways of conveying information to each other. In fact, they are often more powerful than the words we use. We have all been in the position of noticing others say one thing but send a different message by their manner and tone. "It's not so much what she said as the way she said it," we say. A father may express words of praise but, to his son, the words are meaningless if his father barely looks up from his newspaper. Conversely, words of love have a greater impact if accompanied by a hug or a genuine show of interest.

Because parents and children have such a long and intimate history, we might think that good communication comes easily, but the reverse is often true. We grow lazy with those we know well, and sloppy about what we say and how it is delivered. At the same time though, our familiarity makes us more aware of non-verbal cues from those close to us. Facial expressions, sighs, tones of exasperation or pride that might go unnoticed by strangers appear in italics to family members.

Since nothing stands still, parents have to constantly fine tune the content and manner of their communication to fit each child's development. Children pick up cues quickly, sometimes before we are fully aware of them. When very young, children become acutely attuned to any hint of disapproval. When my daughter was a young adult she was quick to point out whenever I repeated any advice. I had thought my suggestion was so subtle that she had missed it. Not so. For her, she was being nagged. She had known for some time what I thought.

The reality is that we cannot *not* communicate. You have probably been part of a group when one person has been silent, apparently taking little interest in what was going on. Like everyone else in the group, you were affected by that person, and speculated about the reason for their silence. Insecure, arrogant, disapproving or, more charitably, shy? In this and many other situations we do not know what another person is feeling, but we cannot help coming to our own conclusions. We may be angry, intimidated or sympathetic, each feeling based on little information. Not surprisingly, we are often mistaken.

Let's look at some common hindrances to effective communication and some techniques to achieve greater clarity.

LISTENING

Of all the components that make up communication, listening is the most valuable. It is an attribute to which we give little thought, taking it for granted, but in truth rarely doing it well. We let words wash over us, hearing the words but not attending to what the other is trying to convey. We are distracted, free associate to parallel situations in our own lives, or rehearse how we want to respond, already forming a judgment before the speaker has finished. Listening is a skill that like all skills we can practice and improve. At its best, it enables us to understand more deeply and so connect with others more fully.

Listening requires attention not just to what is said, but to the other signs that, if we are observant, help us understand what the speaker is attempting to tell us. As we have noted, words not spoken, facial expression, tone of voice, especially when they do not fit the spoken words, all say a great deal. If your daughter asks "Are you coming to us for Thanksgiving this year?" this may be a neutral request for information. Or her tone and emphasis may signal, "As usual, I suppose there's no chance you'll come to us," or "My guess is that you're going to my sister's as you always do." If you sense a hidden meaning in the tone, don't make assumptions: check it out directly with her to keep communications as open and clear as possible

This active listening prevents some of the common communication problems that we all experience, and also cause. How often have you tried to talk to a friend about a problem, only to have her leap in with practical suggestions, or tales of her own experience? Doubtless, you felt misunderstood, frustrated, or even regretful that you had opened the subject. If, on the other hand, another friend gives you her full attention, listens with only the occasional question to help her understand better, you probably have a sense of comfort and support.

As listeners, our goal is to learn what is going on for the person speaking, not how we would react in his place. Suspend any judgment about how he feels or behaves. For most of us, the greatest challenge of good listening is to refrain from suggestions which we think would be helpful but that are, in fact, often misplaced, premature or disrupt the speaker's flow. Our tendency is to address the problem and think about possible solutions, whereas the speaker wants to be heard and understood. The time to voice possible solutions comes later.

At the beginning of my training as a social worker I was sent to see an elderly man who was about to be discharged from the hospital. I knew that his wife had died recently and that he lived alone. He seemed pleased that I was interested in him, his wife's illness and death, and how lonely he felt. Eager to help him, I suggested that the Senior Center might be a resource for him. It was not long before he closed the conversation with a shrug and quick thank-you. My supervisor pointed out what later seemed embarrassingly obvious. I had moved from listening to providing suggestions that the client had shown no sign of wanting. In doing so I had broken the connection we had begun to make. Fortunately for me, there was time and opportunity to correct my clumsiness.

If someone's expression shows that you have not understood him, you can always try again. "Sorry, I didn't quite get it, did I?" Or, if later, you realize you missed his point, "I've been thinking about our conversation of last week, and wanted to ask you more." It's a rare person who is not complimented by your interest, even if your timing was not perfect. Listening is a gift of love. The attention and respect you give, or are given, may be the most important message of all.

HOW TO RESPOND

When someone wants to discuss a problem with you, listening is always the first thing to do. Talking to an interested and empathic person helps most of us feel less oppressed and more able to focus. As a therapist, I often had the opportunity to observe this. A new client spent an hour talking about an emotional issue, such as the illness or death of a loved one and the effect on her, and left saying that she felt lighter and more hopeful. The facts of her life had not changed but her ability to cope with them had increased. Feeling cared about and understood gives us all more resilience to deal with life's knocks.

Then there are times that listening is the only possible response. Everyone goes though difficulties—people die, marriages break up, bodies fail—for which there are no solutions. It is very difficult to watch while those we love are in pain, especially when helpless to change it, but listening, communicating your support and love, does help. Often a gentle touch is worth more than words.

In many instances, listening is the wisest response. As parents, we are so often tempted to give our children advice, because, after all, we have done so for years. But giving unasked for advice is a habit to undo. Parents and children are especially sensitive to advice from each other. They are quick to give it, to resist it, and to resent it. As parents we have probably already given all the advice in our repertoire, so the best approach is to pay attention, ask questions and generally help our children generate solutions that seem right for them. What we think we would do in their place is rarely relevant. Ask yourself how often you have taken another's unsolicited advice unless it agreed with your own thoughts. Not often, I suspect. And your children are no different. The most we can do is to provide opportunities for them to see their situation more clearly.

One of my daughters once asked if it was a burden for me to hear her troubles. I told her that I was sad and concerned for her but not weighed down. I knew she was capable and would find her way. Much later, she told me that my listening and my confidence in her was all she needed.

If there is a place for advice and suggestions it is after you have listened and understood. Then you are better informed and, more important, have shown your support and interest. Wise suggestions are just that, unaccompanied by 'shoulds' and 'oughts.' "Have you thought about….?" is a palatable way of introducing your thoughts.

Concentration on the positive is another tool that helps us communicate usefully. Here I am not talking about focusing on the bright side of life, appropriate though that may be, but the ability to give praise that is personal and specific. "I'm sure everything will be OK" may possibly be helpful, but "I can understand that you are worried but you have a long record of doing well," is more reassuring. We all appreciate positive comments that are well informed and given honestly—and of course they must be both, if they are to be credible.

Many years ago I was part of a class on public speaking. Each of us had a weekly assignment to make a videotape of ourselves giving a three minute talk on a given topic. All the tapes were then played to the entire class. At discussion time our teacher emphasized that we should give only positive feedback. She demonstrated that in her own critique. I still remember how influenced I was by one of her comments to me. "I was happy," she said, "to see you move out from behind the lectern and use your arms more." I have never been immobile in any talk I have given since.

Family relationships are important structures in our lives but they are tender and vulnerable. It seems that we are often less patient and considerate with our family members than with those we know less well. To think that because we are family, we can blurt out whatever occurs to us is a big mistake. It is just because we are important to each other that we are more able to hurt each other. In the same vein we can take others for granted, assuming that they know they are appreciated. We do not hesitate to praise children but often forget to give it to adults. Expressing our admiration and gratitude when appropriate helps all of us, at whatever age, to grow and feel valued.

WHEN TENSIONS OCCUR

Within the fabric of any family there is plenty of opportunity for tensions to arise, and despite good intentions on both sides, children and parents do sometimes quarrel and feel uneasy with each other. Since the variation in human relationships is infinite, it follows that each family is different in its own way. Some families take disagreements in their stride while others simmer angrily. What causes a rift between some relatives may be brushed aside by others. What hurts one member of the family may be greeted with a shrug by another. It is important for our purposes here to define what is a problem for you? What angers or distresses you in your family? What keeps you awake at night? Are the upsets short-lived and easily resolved, or chronic and frequent enough to be a problem? One thing we do know is that the stress-free family does not exist.

First, let me talk about run-of-the-mill tensions. I hesitate to use such a phrase because any matter that causes concern is serious to the worrier. I am not minimizing these anxieties but I am trying to keep them in proportion. Most people know what it is to take a worry and let one's imagination run with it, turning a concern into a problem that in all likelihood may not happen. I know I do this. Someone I love is late getting home. Despite my efforts to remain calm, I have them in the hospital, or worse.

When worry takes over, here are a few helpful points to consider. Do you know that a problem exists, or are you imagining that one will occur? Your daughter has just told you that she's angry with her husband and you leap to thoughts of divorce. Settle back and have a calm look at what is concerning you. You will find that your brain makes many mistakes, and generates thoughts that often have little to do with reality. Remind yourself that thoughts are not facts.

Second, a problem does exist but we imagine it more serious than it is. Again, it is difficult not to do this when we are thinking about a loved one in trouble, but it is helpful to recognize what we are doing. Again, try to stay with the facts rather than the catastrophes created by your imagination. Prospective layoffs at your son's place of work may be a reason for some concern but to project that he will be unemployed, unable to find another job and become financially bankrupt is a vivid imagination. And yet that is what many of us do.

Third, problems sometimes belong to someone other than we thought. A son may be unusually quiet, not because he does not want to be with you, but because he is fretting about his work. Or conversely, you may think that your child has a problem but in reality it belongs to you. I remember one client who was distraught about her daughter's upcoming marriage to a man from a different culture. She was afraid, she said, that life would be too difficult for them. Her daughter protested that she had weighed any potential difficulties and was definite about wanting to marry, and to marry this man. This problem was clearly the mother's, and her's alone. Her reactions, however, were creating difficulties for others and threatening her relationship with her daughter and prospective son-in-law.

When parents see something amiss in the family, they may feel compelled to voice their concerns and give their opinion. At this tender point, I think it wise to be cautious.

Are you are distressed about something that is important? How is your relative likely to react to your comments? Are you returning to an old and well-worn topic? How can you avoid being interpreted as critical? These questions require consideration if you are to maximize your chance of being helpful. If you decide to go ahead, be clear to your children that you want to talk about something you have observed, that bothers you, and that you need to speak about it. Your intent is to help.

When talking to someone about your concerns it is useful to employ what are called 'I messages' By this, I mean that we should be careful to speak about ourselves, avoiding the use of 'you'. As an example, you might say, "I've noticed that you and John don't seem as close these days," rather than "You and John are quarreling a lot these days." This makes what you say less unpalatable, and much more difficult to argue with, because it is not only correct—you are saying what you are thinking or observing—but nor are you blaming or criticizing. Of course, you have no control over how your children react to what you say. If they disagree, become angry, defensive, or brush your concerns aside, let the matter drop. An argument never leads to a constructive exchange of ideas or opinions.

I remember a time when I expressed some concern to my daughter about her impatience with her son, my first grandchild. I thought for a long while about whether to say anything, and, if so, when and how I would say it. I felt strongly that something needed to be said and that only her mother would say it. I took considerable pains to acknowledge the stress she was under and that the perceptions were mine, but despite my care, she felt criticized, misunderstood and let down by someone she considered her chief ally. I doubt that my intervention was constructive. Would I do the same again? Possibly, but I would be more careful in my choice of time and place.

When quarrels occur, each of us is convinced that not only are we right, but also that we need our rightness to be recognized. Remember that it takes two egos to argue. Meanwhile you have some choices. You can foster an unpleasant situation by returning a sharp or critical rejoinder. You can choose to defend yourself, which is not usually productive. You can deflect a potential argument by ignoring what happened, change the subject or even leave the room. You can return to the contentious subject at a calmer time. Or you can consider a response which side steps a potential argument by agreeing with what the other said. If greeted with "You're always late," you might reply, "That's true" (if it is true), or say, "I certainly am today. Sorry." Then there is nothing to argue about and bad feelings evaporate quickly.

Within families, conflicts can be difficult to resolve, rooted as they are in patterns of reaction and behavior built over many years. Old habits and feelings tend to come to the surface especially when children visit their parents or siblings. Minor irritations, fueled by our personal history, may escalate until they are out of proportion to the matter at hand. When a problem occurs, we tend to behave as we always have. We argue, withdraw, reason, get angry, all of which we have tried many times before, without success.

If we are stuck in an uncomfortable or unproductive pattern, one thing we know is that our usual ways of handling situations do not work. It's time to try something new. And the only person to do that is oneself. Finding fault with others and thinking that they are the ones to change brings nothing but resentment and frustration. If we can nurture understanding and tolerance within ourselves, however, we may see others respond positively to the difference in us. In close relationships, a shift in one often leads to a change in the other, and it can be in a good direction.

SETTING LIMITS

For the most part, the atmosphere in our family is probably one of mutual support, in which affection and sense of responsibility wins over personal convenience. Boundaries are broader and more flexible than they are in most other relationships. Honesty is a sound basis for any connection, however. There is something amiss if we find ourselves saying "yes" and resenting it. Our irritation will spill over, spoiling the encounter for everyone. We have the need and the right to draw limits around what we chose to do, and not do.

I gave some thought to this issue of boundaries a few years ago when my daughter and family moved to live much closer to me. I was delighted. The prospect of seeing her more often and of being a significant part of my grandchildren's lives thrilled me. At the same time, I realized I did not want to spend all my time with them. I love the company of my grandchildren but I also have many other activities and occupations that that are important to me. Doubtless, it would have been easier for my daughter if I were a baby-sitting kind of grandmother, but we have worked out our respective needs to the satisfaction of us all.

We cannot expect our children to read our minds. It is our responsibility to speak up if we do not want our grandchildren playing with our kitchen pans, or using our beds as trampolines. It is our home and we are allowed to have some rules. It is fair, though, to make sure that everyone is clear about them. My parents had a rule for themselves that they would never correct their grandchildren while their parents were present. (A good practice, I thought). Unfortunately they failed to let their children know they did not want the grandchildren climbing on their furniture. In the exuberance of family visits I forgot to recognize that my parents might have different standards than I. It was only later that I learned that my father had been annoyed that I had not reined in my children. I remember wishing that he had said something at the time instead of holding on to his resentment.

DIFFICULT TOPICS

The extent to which members of families discuss their problems varies considerably. Some parents and children are very close, sharing most of their concerns. Even in our mobile society many women list their mother or daughter among their closest friends. They talk frequently, and support each other physically and emotionally. Other parents and children, also close, keep to everyday and practical subjects.

Are you content with how much your children tell you? Would you like them to confide in you when they are troubled? If you would like to be more included, you can show your interest by the occasional question. If your child fails to elaborate, however, assume he does not want to talk and drop the matter.

It may be that your children tell you more than you want to know. Most of us like to feel included and with any luck, to feel useful, but the down side is that our worries may affect our sleep and sense of wellbeing. A friend told me of a significant change that had taken place as she reached her 80s. For decades she had thrived on being the matriarch of her large family. Everyone told her their troubles and sought her advice. Now she wanted to hear about difficulties only when they were over.

Often the mother is the communication center talking to the children regularly and passing on news about each to the others. This informal system usually works well if mothers are careful to relay only neutral information and keep any confidences or opinions to themselves. Good and bad news are for the owner to share. I have known mothers who act as a go-between in their children's relationships. Eager to help them like each other, they become secret mediators, explaining one child to another and suggesting how each might behave. Such attempts though well meaning invariably backfire, leaving all concerned angry and resentful. I knew one woman who alienated her grandchildren because she lectured them constantly about how they should include their lonely mother in their social life.

As parents, how much do we tell our children about our problems? While we are relatively young most us probably confide less in our children than they do in us. We are too much the parent to want to discuss our emotional issues with them, or even to feel it is appropriate. Over time our needs may change, as does our children's maturity. Parents who are widowed or have a disabled spouse are more likely to talk to their children about personal matters. And their children are usually pleased that they do so. They will worry more if they are not kept in the loop. As adults they do not need to be protected from problems and may have something useful to contribute.

In this age of psychiatry many of you have or will have children who seek help from therapists. This can be a puzzling experience for parents who have learned to keep emotional matters to themselves. More painfully you may suspect that you are a subject of discussion and even criticism during your child's sessions. Your child may ask you difficult questions about the past, be angry, or distant; meanwhile you may feel guilty, misunderstood or unappreciated.

Not all children have perfect childhoods. Many have to deal with unhappy parents, illness, disrupted families, or even abuse. In adulthood some people want to understand more about what has happened to them and how they can handle the emotional repercussions more comfortably. How they recall their past may make little sense to you. You may not remember incidents that were vivid to them, and if you do, your memory of them is likely to be different. It is vital, however, that you respect that their feelings are valid for them. It is rare that two members of a family have similar recollections, and certainly not the same emotional reactions to the same event. What is important is that your child is trying to sort her feelings about her past and how she can live more easily in the present. It may be a lengthy process but if she benefits, so will you all.

HUMOR

Families see each other at their best and their worst, at their happiest and their saddest, at their most relaxed and their most tense. If we are wise, we are slow to take offense and do not take everything seriously.

Let me end with a word of appreciation for humor. It is a balm that makes it easier to say difficult things and also to hear them. A gentle, good-natured manner can make the difference between someone being responsive to your remarks or upset by them. Of all human attributes, humor has the power to warm and lighten our interactions.

POINTS TO CONSIDER

- Communication is made up of many components—words, tone of voice, facial expression, body language.

- Listening is an invaluable skill, helping us to fully understand what another person is trying to convey. It is also a gift of interest and respect to the speaker.

- Be careful about giving unsolicited advice.

- When talking about your concerns to anyone use 'I' rather than 'you'. For example. "I'm worried about the amount you seem to be drinking" versus "You are drinking too much." That way you avoid being judgmental or critical.

- Good communication does not mean that we always agree with each other but it does mean that we try to understand and respect the validity of each other's opinions.

- If you are worried about an event that has occurred in

your family try to think calmly about your reaction. Are you concerned about something that is not a problem—yet? Is your imagination running amok? Are you sad rather than worried because the problem has no solution? Does the problem belong to you rather than another family member? The answer might help you.

- Keep a sense of humor. It lightens almost any situation.

Family Expansion

Sooner or later your family will expand again, this time to include strangers. Unlike friends, the partners, spouses and offspring of your children are not chosen by you, but they do become part of your family. Given the variety of humankind and the complexity of relationships some of the newcomers bring pleasure, others are a challenge, and most are a combination of the two. Keeping the family balanced and more or less congenial with each addition requires tolerance and generosity from everyone. Parents, especially, want all family members to enjoy each other. There are ways you can both help and hinder family accord.

IN-LAWS
The first to arrive are your sons-in-law and daughters-in-law. When two young people are thinking of marrying, meeting each other's parents is an important step. So much hinges on how each reacts to the other. If you are fortunate, you will like your child's prospective partner and be delighted that he or she may join your family. "She's a joy and we're looking forward to her being one of us," one friend said of his future daughter-in-law. But reactions are not always so positive. You may have reservations. "He's a nice person but I don't think he has enough energy or ambition for her." On occasion, parents actively dislike their child's

choice. "She makes no effort to get to know us. In fact I'm sure she tries to keep him away from us."

Whatever your first impressions, give any newcomer the benefit of the doubt. It is not easy being introduced to a new group of people, all of whom know each other well and are scrutinizing you as a prospective addition to the family. Under such circumstances few of us are at our best. Spend time together before you decide that this alliance is doomed or that you can never like this potential son-in-law or daughter-in-law.

At some level many of us believe that nobody is quite good enough for our children. We want the best for them, forgetting that our best is almost certainly not the same as theirs.

Certainly our own parents had their list of negative attributes that would worry them in a future spouse for their children. Then misgivings tended to revolve around religion, history of divorce, or a child out of wedlock. Now such concerns can seem rather quaint and irrelevant. We all have our own prejudices. Accepting that our child has chosen someone of a different race or of the same sex may give us pause. When presented with the unfamiliar, especially in our own family, many of us act with a distinct lack of enthusiasm, even disapproval. "He seems perfectly nice but I can't get used to the idea," we may say. "She is so different that I can't imagine we'll ever find anything to talk about." Be patient and keep your mind open. In time, you will probably see the person beneath the surface and find much to like.

When a son marries, his mother may have strong feelings about being replaced as the most important woman in his life. A father may have similar reactions to the introduction of his daughter's chosen husband. These are difficult feelings to recognize in ourselves, but if you have a problem getting on with your children's partners it is worth considering whether it stems, at least in part, from your sense of personal loss. And of course there is some loss. Your children are taking an important step when they form their own families. As parents we have to accept that our young adult's natural course is to create a new primary relationship, and that cannot happen if we remain top priority.

When your children form relationships that are clearly serious, you are all on tender ground. You are dying to know what your children are thinking and feeling but may hesitate to ask, waiting for them to make the first move. Much will depend on your relationship and your individual personalities. Some children use their parents as confidantes, others keep their own counsel. You know them well enough to follow their lead, but do so with care. For instance, if they ask what you think about their new love you have to judge whether they are unsure about their own minds and are genuinely seeking your opinion, or whether they know what they think and just want your seal of approval. If they have some doubts, ask for their thoughts and listen carefully. When you speak, do so honestly but gently. If they are sure about their decision, but you are not, restrain yourself from being forceful or lengthy about your reservations. After all they know this person much better than you do.

Giving unsolicited advice is a delicate process at the best of times. If your child is in love, it is probably worse than useless. If your disapproval is so strong that you must speak out, do it as thoughtfully and as lovingly as you can. Express what you like about the person as well as your concerns, all the while recognizing that any decision is not yours to make. State your impressions and thoughts, using "I" to make clear that you are describing your own observations. These "I" messages were touched on in the previous chapter but seem worth repeating here. "I'm concerned about the amount he drinks" is more effective than, "He drinks too much." If you talk in terms of 'you', 'he', or 'she' you will invite an argument or at least a defensive protest. If you speak for yourself, your child may disagree with you but is less likely to build a wall between you. Unless he or she shows a willingness to talk let the matter drop, knowing that to persist would be a mistake.

Should you continue to find a child's partner difficult, you do not have to fall over backwards to be best friends, but you do have to be pleasant. It is never fair to complain to your children about their spouse or implicitly ask them to choose between spouse and parents. It is a competition you can never win. If your children have to pick one over the other they will stand by the person with whom they have chosen to spend their life.

One woman came to see me about her daughter-in-law with whom she had had a negative relationship for many years. She never phoned her son at home "because I can't bring myself to be nice to his wife if she answers." For the same reason she never visited his home. Her son went alone to see her. She was adamant that her daughter-in-law needed to make an apology for a perceived slight that had happened at their wedding many years ago. She seemed to be saying that it would be dishonest to be pleasant to someone she disliked for allegedly wronging her.

Fortunately this level of dissension is not common but there are plenty of people who do not much like their in-laws. That is not surprising since we do not select them, but wise parents make it their business to get on with their children's spouses. They know that affection may not be possible but being congenial is. One client described how she succeeded in forming a positive, if not intimate, relationship with her son's wife. It was not easy from the beginning. The newcomer had many characteristics that she found irritating, and they had no interests in common. My client asked herself two questions. "Do I want my son to be happy?" "Does his wife make him happy?" The answer to both questions was "Yes." So they did have something in common. In supporting their marriage and working to create some bond with her daughter-in-law this woman can now enjoy short visits.

I cannot stress how vital it is to tolerate our children's partners, and to do so with grace. If we fail to be gracious and welcoming we will create an untenable situation for our child and a tension between us.

At a greater distance but still relevant is the family of your child's spouse—your child's in-laws. For you, this relationship may be emotionally neutral, but you will come into contact on big family events and small ones if you live nearby. In the interests of harmony any incipient competition between you—that for the grandchildren is a common one—should be kept under wraps.

Soon after deciding to live together a couple has to decide how to relate to each other's family. The awkward introductory visits are over, preliminary impressions formed, but the work has only just begun. Children, just like their parents, hope they will like and even come to love their new family. If they are not so fortunate, they too have to determine to be friendly and considerate.

How close adult children are to their respective parents depends on many factors, including geography, ability to travel and affection. Most children do try to be fair to both sets of parents. You help your children a great deal if you can be sensitive to their ties with their other family, and accept that on occasion you have to share your son or daughter.

Competing relationships tend to come to a head at the holidays. How to satisfy everyone? Couples may agonize over plans and arrangements, and travel long distances in order to give equal time to both families. Early in our marriage, my husband and I almost checked our watches during our Christmas visits to our parents. They lived within a mile of each other and we speculated that they counted how many hours we spent and how many meals we ate with the other.

My brother and his wife solved the "Christmas problem" by suggesting that they and their children and grandchildren celebrate the holiday on a weekend early in December, leaving the 25–26th free for their children to visit the other parents. This has now become their tradition.

Only too often, children feel that their parents' holiday traditions are set in stone, and that any change would hurt many feelings. At times, though, some might want to break with the traditional family visit. Parents of young children might prefer to stay home. Childless couples might want to use their precious time off for travel. Families with older children might choose a physically active venue. And sometimes it is we older parents who want to avoid the festive scene for once! But we all hesitate to suggest a different plan.

As the important holidays approach, the media is full of the stress of the season. It is expectations that bring the most angst. Most of us are skilled at assuming that everyone else is a member of a loving, fun-loving family that enjoys nothing so much as several days spent together. Doubtless some families are like that but many get to the point of wanting to alter the pattern, at least on occasion. It is possible to make a tradition of evaluating the tradition. It just takes someone brave enough to test the waters and then open a discussion.

GRANDCHILDREN

Grandchildren are one of the joys of having adult children. Many people find the relationship with their grandchildren more enjoyable and certainly more relaxed than with their own children when young. Most of us do not have the awesome responsibility of raising our grandchildren, but are able to choose when and how long they stay with us. As for the grandchildren, they relish the unconditional love and attention from adults whose main goal is to give them a good time.

In addition to being an enormous satisfaction in their own right, the presence of grandchildren sometimes brings older parents closer to their own children. With motherhood in common, mothers and daughters may understand each other better and appreciate the love they share for the babies. Meanwhile older men often enjoy spending more time with grandchildren than was available to them when their own children were little. Their sons and daughters may watch this loving or playful aspect of their father with new appreciation.

Rarely in family life does everything go smoothly. So it is where grandchildren are concerned—or rather, where grandchildren and their parents are concerned. The older generation relishes the affection they give to and receive from their grandchildren, they play games and read aloud, enjoy introducing the children to new experiences, and boast about their intelligence and cuteness. It can be a precious relationship. Nevertheless, at times, we may deplore the way our grandchildren are raised. For some of us, they have no manners, no discipline and are over-indulged. Or we may think they have onerous pressures put on them and lead lives that have too many restrictions and too little freedom. Our children will doubtless have different rules for their offspring than we had for them. They may be much looser about bedtimes than we were, or perhaps they have no such thing as a sit-down family meal. On consideration, however, many of the behaviors we observe and criticize are neither right nor wrong, merely different.

Love and joy are easy to express but how do we handle our disapproval or concern? What do we say as our grandchildren refuse to go to bed until 10.00 pm, watch hours of television, or are not allowed to eat the snacks we bring. The answer is: nothing. We may think we are making a tactful comment about our grandchildren's behavior or routine but to our children any implicit criticism is loud and clear. We cannot fail to have our opinions, but it is best to keep them to ourselves. The blunt fact is, it is none of our business how our children rear their children. The painful exception to this fact occurs if we suspect child abuse, in which case, of course, we have to report it. In general, though, there are many good ways to raise children, and our children, as we did, do their best.

Change is constant whether in child rearing, pace of life or standard of living. Each generation brings up its young in a world different from the one in which their parents raised them. As parents we may have expectations for our children that they not only do not fill, but may have no wish or ability to do so. A mother from a generation when almost all mothers worked only in the home, may deplore that her grandchildren are in day care, but she will only alienate her daughter if she hints that her daughter has made a bad choice. We parents are the ones who have to adapt to, or at least, tolerate the differences. Looking at the dangers and problems with which today's parents are now beset, I know I would not change places with them.

How do you act when your grandchildren are in your care and your home? You can certainly have your own rules. Children can cope with different rules in different places— they do so in school everyday—so you are not making life difficult for them if your rules differ from those in their home. What we must avoid is undermining their parents by suggesting our rules are superior, rather than merely our personal choice.

Some grandparents who read this may be in the position of seeing little of their grandchildren. Perhaps they live far away, or there has been a rift in the family, or poor health makes travel difficult. In all probability, however, you are an important person to your grandchildren though you see each other rarely. Letters, gifts, telephone conversations, and email for the older ones, fill the gap somewhat. Unfortunately your grandchildren may not respond. They require a motivated adult to help them maintain contact and not all adults will make that effort. If you can persevere with the occasional present or card, your grandchild may respond when he is able to make the effort on his own behalf.

DIVORCE

It is a rare family that does not experience a breakup of the marriage of at least one of its members. As divorce has become a common occurrence in our culture, parents are less apt to blame themselves for the failure of their child's marriage, but it is still an upsetting time for everyone. Divorce can be a seismic shift within the family.

When your child's marriage ends you will probably have a mixture of feelings. Shock may be the first. The state of other people's marriages is often a well-kept secret. I know I have been surprised by the news that friends are separating. "How did I not see that coming?" "Why didn't they say they were in trouble?" So it may be with your children. Troubled couples often do not want to talk to anyone, except each other, while they are trying to work things out. In particular they may hesitate to worry their parents before they have to.

When my husband and I decided to divorce, we did not tell our parents until we were clear about our plan. Speaking for myself, I know I was not prepared to deal with the many inevitable questions. I knew my parents would not be critical of me but they might be of my husband and that would bring no comfort to me. Living on different continents, it was easy to keep my distress to myself and I told myself there was little they could do anyway. When I broke the news to them they were so warm and concerned that I realized I was wrong to believe that there was nothing they could do.

Other feelings flood in depending on the circumstances of the couple's breakup. You may be angry if one of them seems to have behaved badly, you may worry about grandchildren, or you may even feel relief if you have been watching an unsatisfactory marriage unravel for too long. Whatever the circumstances, you will certainly feel sad for the loss of hopes and dreams that accompany the end of any relationship.

Whenever you hear about a child's marital difficulties your first concern must be for the couple and especially your own child. How are they doing? How are their children reacting? How can I help? Your questions about the "why's" and "how's" can wait. For your child, it is your love that he or she needs to feel.

After the first impact, there will be other questions. How will your son-in-law or daughter-in-law fit into your life? How do you want him or her to do so? For many grandparents, the most vital personal question is how this divorce will affect their relationship with their grandchildren.

Divorce creates a legal separation between a husband and wife but can also create a rift between two families. The divorcing couple has to deal with each other in order to untangle their lives. If they have children, their contact with each other is likely to be long term. There are no rules for the other family members, however, many of whom may rarely see each other again. What about parents who were close to their former son-in-law or daughter in-law? And what about grandparents whose grandchildren now spend most of their time with a former in-law?

There are innumerable post-divorce arrangements, each requiring tact, goodwill and above all the capacity in the adults concerned to hold the welfare of the children as their first priority.

One client was dismayed when her son ended his marriage by falling love with another woman. Her daughter-in-law had the custody of the two young children, and my client wanted to maintain contact with her. Her son was not happy about her decision. She, however, had always enjoyed a warm relationship with her daughter-in-law and wanted to sustain it for herself and her grandchildren. By supporting each estranged partner and grandchild, she was able to keep a relationship with them all.

BLENDED FAMILIES
It is a fact of our times that the majority of families do not fit the traditional near universal structure of mother, father and their biological children. Today all of us know families with single parents, with divorced parents, children living with step- or adopted parents, parents of different races or the

same gender. Children may spend time in two homes with different parents, children in the same home may have different parents, and children may have as many as four sets of grandparents.

It is not easy to raise children under any circumstances but being a single parent or part of a couple raising children from previous marriages presents special challenges. They will all need your help and support. And you have to decide how to incorporate grandchildren who share no blood with you.

For most of us, love does not come immediately when we meet a child unrelated to us. It takes time to grow. And circumstances can help or hinder that growth. The subject of step-grandchildren arose when I was with a group of friends recently. We all had different experiences. One of my daughters helps to raise her husband's daughter who splits her time between her mother's and her father's homes. Early in their marriage I did not see her often because she was at school or with her mother. She was also too shy to be friendly. With time we have become fond of each other and she is an enjoyable part of the family.

One member of the group was puzzled to know how to deal with her son's two stepchildren. Whenever they visit their mother they return laden with gifts, upsetting her son's young daughter. My friend's inclination was to indulge her granddaughter so as to even out the total number of gifts received. Others thought that they would rather treat all three children more or less evenly rather than compensate one for having fewer relatives than the others.

Another woman has rarely seen her step-grandchild since the parents' divorce because the child's natural mother makes every effort to keep her son away from his step-father and his family.

The last person to speak said that her first grandchild was a step-, the son of her son-in-law. Her son-in-law had lost his wife to cancer so my friend's daughter had a full-time child, as well as a husband, on their wedding day. The young boy found it hard to adjust to a new mother, and made it clear that he did not like her. In the early difficult months, he was much more able to accept affection from his step-grandmother rather than a replacement for his mother. With time he formed a strong bond with his stepmother; the warm relationship with his step-grandmother remained.

Circumstances vary greatly and so do our relationships with step-grandchildren. Situations change over time and generally grow more comfortable as children and adults get to know each other and the new family constellation. It is important that we remember we are dealing with children. They have to deal with the divorce of their parents, new relatives, the division of their time between different homes— changes beyond their control and rarely ones they are happy about. With patience and understanding, parents and children settle into their new situation, feel comfortable and even grow to love each other.

A PARENT RE-MARRIES
Should you decide to remarry, the waves within your family will be extensive, especially among your children. Your children are adult but you are still their parent and they will almost certainly have strong feelings about your new relationship, whether it follows a divorce or a death. They have

to accommodate to you living with a relative stranger whom they also have to fit into their lives. With time, they will be reconciled if they see you happy with a new partner and, at best, may come to enjoy the new member of the family. Before that happens, however, many children receive the news as an unpleasant shock.

Your children will have many concerns and questions. I am not suggesting you even hint that you want their approval before making your decision, but for the sake of your relationship, you do want to hear what they have to say. They may be afraid that you are being taken advantage of, or that their inheritance will disappear. They may feel you are betraying their deceased parent especially if the death was recent. They may have concerns about your prospective partner, feeling that you are settling for too little. Or if you and your child have a close relationship, especially if it became closer since you were widowed, your child may regard your new spouse as an unwelcome intrusion. Some of your children's concerns may have some foundation, some not, but they are all worth airing.

Try to understand their reactions. If they seem angry and selfish in their concerns know that this is a common reaction to loss, and time will make a big difference. When one of my friends told his daughter that he was remarrying, she said, "I'm sure she's a perfectly nice lady but I don't need another nice lady in my life."

At some time talk about your own feelings. Your children may not fully realize that despite your affection for them and your grandchildren you are often lonely and long for a compatible companion of your own.

For you too your new relationship brings challenges. One of them is balancing your wish to give time and energy to another person with maintaining your contact with your children and grandchildren. One of my clients was upset when her mother, with whom she was close emotionally and geographically, left with her new husband in a camper on an indefinite trip around the Americas. Her mother flew home for family occasions but for many months my client felt the loss of her company.

However happily newcomers are absorbed into a family there is no rule that members of the original family only see each other in the company of spouses. Most parents like to see their children alone on occasion and vice versa. It is not a sign that you have secrets or you dislike someone, it is a natural impulse. I am fond of both my daughters' spouses but I enjoy spending time alone with the girls. If you remarry, it may be especially important for you and your partner to be open on occasion to seeing your own children without the other.

It may be that one or other of you may not much like your spouses' children. Or you may like them well enough but do not want to put energy into creating close relationships with more adult children. Conflict in second marriages often occurs around the children that do not belong to both partners. And the children do not have to be young to be the source of dissension. You may make more excuses for, be more tolerant of, and show more interest in your children than your new partner ever will. If he or she is critical of your children you will probably leap to their defense, even as you realize that you partially agree with the criticism. When this happens, try an experiment. If you do think your partner has a point, tell her so. Then the argument never starts. The best course of action is to be as tolerant as possible—of your stepchildren and your spouse.

Even long-married couples may regard visits of their children with different degrees of pleasure or patience. No new partner, however wonderful in many ways, will love your children as you do. And you cannot assume that he or she will welcome your children using your house as their own, or staying for long periods.

If you or your spouse dislike any of the other's children, or as adult children you do not like your parent's new partner, you all have to behave in a civil fashion. Maintaining a comfortable relationship with the people who are important to you requires that you are all thoughtful and considerate towards each other.

POINTS TO CONSIDER

- Sooner or later your family will expand to include strangers—your children's spouses, partners and grandchildren. It will be important to you that everyone enjoys each other. Though you cannot make that happen you can do much to help or hinder family congeniality.

- Whatever your impressions of your child's prospective partner, give him or her the benefit of the doubt and time to get to know each other.

- If you dislike or disapprove of your child's choice of mate remember that it is not your decision to make. Unless you are asked for your opinion, keep thoughts to yourself. If asked, be honest but gentle.

- Regardless of your feelings it is vital that you tolerate your in-laws, and do so with grace. To do otherwise risks family discord and hurts those you love.
- In all likelihood your children raise their children differently than you did them. Not right or wrong, but different. The world has changed a great deal since you were a young adult, and your children are probably more capable of helping their youngsters negotiate it than you are.
- If you remarry, you cannot expect your spouse to love your children as you do. Relations with children can be a flashpoint in second marriages. Tolerance and compassion are called for.

When Things Fall Apart

The term, "The Golden Years," was probably invented by an advertising agency, not by someone over the age of 75. Although much about old age is enjoyable and ful-filling, those who have reached that stage are increasingly aware that their self-reliance and strength are finite. While healthy, most older people revel in their increased leisure and relative freedom from responsibility, and with any luck have a great deal to enjoy and many years to do so. They and their children know, however, that their minds and bodies are, or will be, less dependable than they used to be. At first, these changes are often in-significant, except as warning signals, but they become more difficult to dismiss. Jokes about forgetfulness and "senior moments" are as predictable as the anxiety that they attempt to conceal. Alert to any sign of diminish-ment, both parents and children may give exaggerated weight to every memory slip or moment of confusion. Whether real or imagined, diminished capacities herald another shift that affects parents and their families.

Yet humans can be amazingly resilient. We are able to adapt to all kinds of change and still live our lives relying mostly on our own resources. We use aids to compensate for diminished eyesight, hearing and balance; we find help with heavy housework and gardening; and we move to a smaller house. We do not like much of it but we do stay more or less in charge. It is that sense of control that is important.

The overwhelming majority of old people—at least in our culture—say that their greatest fear is being dependent. For most, the dependence they dread is the necessity of turning to others for the kind of care that they have always regarded as their own responsibility. So those who have always attended to their own house or garden, and now cannot quite cope, may fiercely deny any hint that they need to employ outside help . Past fantasies about someone to assist with chores may lose their attraction when children suggest that "the time" may have come. Parents protest and, not rarely, refuse. It's the need to accept help that is unacceptable.

Parents' resistance may drive their adult children crazy. And they have a point. But more on that later.

The reality is that sooner or later, most of us cannot be totally sufficient unto ourselves. Barring sudden death we will need to depend on others. This shift may come suddenly with the appearance of a stroke, for example, or it may creep up at a gradual pace. However it comes, you and your children have new, difficult questions to face. Your need for help adds a new element to your relationship. One of my older clients realized that, as she put it, "I've become a project. I see my children huddling together and know that they're conferring on how Mom is doing."

As old people begin to lose their capacities, almost without realizing it, they look more to their children to fill in the gaps. And their children expect that they will respond—as far as possible. They also suspect that at some point their parents' needs may exceed the ability of the family to fill, and that they will have to employ outside services.

Families have always been the chief support system for their own members and probably always will be. Despite the growth in social services and community programs, it is families who continue to provide the majority of the care. Though we hear much about the decline in family values, the overwhelming evidence is that children choose to care for, and about, their elderly relatives. Even the small number of parents who elect to move into a continuing care facility, designed specifically to meet all the social, housing, personal care and health needs of old people from fitness to sickness to death, continue to look to their children for the personal help and interest no institution can provide.

This chapter focuses on the time when things begin to fall apart, when the changes in ourselves and those we love affect our lives in significant ways, when losses are permanent, and sometimes severe enough to turn our world upside down. When this happens, we will face a difficult task which takes patience and courage. This is the stage of life when the phrase, "Old age is not for sissies," is so often quoted.

WHAT IS GOING ON FOR YOU?
Our bodies can fall apart at any time in our lives, but in old age deterioration is a natural occurrence. Unless we die young and quickly, which most of us hope not to do, we must expect to lose some of our capacities before we die. Losses come in many shapes and forms—physical, emotional and mental—but for the most part they occur slowly,

giving us time to adapt, and, if we are fortunate, our life is not dramatically altered. We allow more time to do everything, accept that we need help with certain tasks, give up driving after dark, and in general adjust our way of living with some complaints but little anguish.

Amazing as it seems to the young, most old people think of themselves as younger and healthier than their contemporaries. "Poor old thing," my 97-year-old mother says of someone younger than she is, and then laughs when she realizes what she has said. I was in a bookstore recently when, handing my purchase to the young cashier, I mentioned that it was a gift for my mother. Surprised, the young man looked up and exclaimed: "You have a mother?" Then it was my turn to be taken aback. Am I old enough for someone to be surprised that I have a living mother? The answer is yes.

I often find it uplifting to work with old people, and to experience how, despite their losses, most of them continue to find satisfaction in their lives. I hear, for example, elderly clients describe some small incident—a smile, a conversation that "made my day." The enforced slower pace of their days provides opportunities that younger, busier lives crowd out. I remember a conversation I had at the senior center where a woman described her brief walk each day "to see how the tree at the end of my street is doing." Here are lessons for us all, regardless of age. I asked a neighbor recently how much she missed her farm, now that she had moved into a smaller house in the village. Yes, she missed it, she said, but she no longer finds pleasure in the heavy work involved in caring for animals, dealing with snow and a bad road, and is ready to enjoy walks and the pace of her simpler home. So, though old age brings aches and pains, and the threat of loss and ill-health, most of us are adaptable enough to discover that there is much to enjoy in life.

Since your children became adults, contacts with each other have been determined largely by affection, opportunity, and geography; and conversation is probably dominated by activities, plans, grandchildren and friends. Now that you are older, the children begin to ask about your health and how you are managing. They have questions, some voiced, some not. "Is the house too much?" "Can you still manage?" "Will you accept help?" And for themselves, "What needs to be done and how can I do it?" And you too have thoughts and questions. You want to be self-sufficient. You want visits and conversations with your children to be enjoyable, not dominated by difficulties and worries.

With these changes come tensions at times. Invariably, your ideas about problems, and even more so about solutions, differ from those of your children. And theirs will differ from each other. Looking ahead to the day when you can no longer care for yourself, your children may feel compelled to plan for that now. Thinking that you are doing well enough at present, you, on the other hand, would rather not look ahead to an uncertain and rather frightening future. Meanwhile, you feel pushed and managed. I am not suggesting that you unthinkingly agree with your children—not with their suggestions or even their worries. They have no first claim to wisdom anymore than you do. They know you, however, and care about you so their observations and opinions are worth listening to and considering. At the very least, your children will appreciate that you are prepared to hear them; at best, you will participate in a conversation that will be of help to you in the future. Questions such as "Isn't it time to give up driving?" "Do you ever think of moving house?" are queries that show concern and deserve a thoughtful discussion where all opinions are aired and heard.

WHAT IS GOING ON FOR YOUR CHILDREN?

As children, when you see your parents becoming sick or frail, you too enter a new stage of your lives. And you will experience a range of feelings. How you react to their needs depends on many factors, practical and emotional. You will be sad, anxious and apprehensive about what this means for you and them, and grieve at the reminder that you will eventually lose them. Some of your feelings will be uncomfortable. You may be upset that their need has come at an inconvenient time, or irritated that they did not follow your advice in caring for themselves or in planning for this day. Such feelings may never get talked about because your concern for your parents far surpasses your other feelings. Anger, jealousy, resentment and other negative emotions are uncomfortable, but they are part of being human. The challenge for all of us is to handle them so that we do not act on them and hurt others.

Life expectancy has changed dramatically over the past fifty years. Most children now expect their parents to reach advanced old age, and may have two, three or even four elderly parents and in-laws for whom they have some responsibility. Plenty of children are themselves elderly, looking out for parents who are very old. Another relevant demographic change is that families have become smaller. The result is that there are fewer children caring for more elderly parents. Finally, while on the subject of trends that affect aging families, most women now work outside the home, and so they add caregiving to a life that is already oversubscribed. "Will I help?" is invariably answered positively. But the question that requires more thought is, "How can I manage to provide my parents with what they need?" Assisting others comes at a cost. Somehow, time, energy and resources have to be found in a life where all are in short supply.

For much of your lives together, you have known that you could turn to your parents for support and guidance. There comes a time, though, when you have more energy, strength and ability to deal with the complexities of a confusing world than they do. Now you are adult, and they are the ones needing help. The tide of suggestions, advice and practical help is flowing more from you to them. These changes are probably not entirely welcome to either of you. Your parents will probably feel grateful, but at times, will also feel diminished, misunderstood, and confused. You will have many reactions too—frustration, fear that you will upset them, and apprehension about how to word your concerns.

Despite everything you will find much to appreciate, even if this stage of life sometimes seems dominated by loss. I was talking with a client recently who is struggling with her sadness and guilt that she had to move her mother to live in a nursing home near her and her family. Her mother has no awareness that she was no longer safe living in her own home. As far as she was concerned she had been moved unnecessarily and against her will. I asked my client if there was anything positive for her in this painful situation. She said that she knew she had done the loving thing, even if her mother did not. She wants to help her mother through this last stage of her life and for her children to be part of their grandmother's life. As her mother slowly adjusts, my client is seeing signs that her mother is more content and that the two of them may have a closer relationship than they have had for decades. Whatever motivates you to help your parents—love, duty, gratitude or any other consideration—you too will be fulfilling an important, and I hope, ultimately satisfying task.

EVALUATE

When I first mentioned that I was considering writing about elderly parents and their relationship with their adult children, several friends expressed the hope that I could persuade their parents to plan for their old age. And would I be quick about it! Though the details varied, friends' experiences and concerns had themes in common. "My parents are beginning to have some health problems and can't manage as they are for much longer. But I can't get them to even think about moving from their home or employing some help. Do we have to wait for a crisis? I'd sooner think about these things ahead of time, but getting them to do that is a different matter."

In my seventies myself, I can understand older peoples' reluctance to contemplate a declining future. But as a therapist and a daughter, I know it is a good idea to evaluate our living situation every so often. Perhaps it is worth getting into that habit before we need help.

At present I feel light years away from having to turn to others for personal help, but when I'm honest I notice some changes in myself. And the changes are not in the direction of gaining strength and stamina. What does that mean in practice? Not much at present. But it will. Occasionally I let myself think about my old age, or, at least, what old age may bring me. Will I be able to stay in this house if I can't drive? Under what conditions could I imagine living in an assisted living facility? I certainly don't need help from my children at present but perhaps I should help them with the reality of my aging? After all, they have never been older than they are now and so have no knowledge of what it is like to be in an older body.

Looking in the opposite direction, and one that concerns me more at present, I certainly want my mother to let me know how she is doing and what help she needs and when. Like many families, my siblings and I discuss her well-being at length, but we are hesitant about raising with her the possibilities we all fear. What if she can no longer live alone? Our mother too is reluctant to engage in a conversation that has the potential to upset or frighten her. Any foray into such topics quickly ends with her saying, "Well, I don't want to be a nuisance to my children and I pray I'll never have to go to a nursing home. Let's hope it never comes to that. Now let's talk about something more cheerful." And there is a sigh of relief from us all that she is doing just fine at present.

There are many reasons not to think about the future when we are old. "Why depress myself?" " I'm too busy with the present." "Who knows what the future holds anyway?" And children are almost as reluctant. "The time never seems right." "They're doing so well, why rock the boat?" All true, but it makes sense to review the present living arrangements on occasion, and, to include each other in the conversation. Are the parents safe, comfortable and receiving the help they need? And the children, are they satisfied with the existing circumstances? Are they easy in their minds about their parents and about their ability to contribute to their care?

Even if the situation is stable, a review gives everyone a chance to anticipate a time when a change might be necessary. One of the difficulties of old age is that we can rarely know what will happen, or when. Unless we decide ahead of time that the comprehensive care of a retirement community is what we want, it is difficult to make plans. There are just too many unknowns. I have plenty of sympathy for older people for whom any projected change is invariably unwelcome, and so find it easier to hope it will never be necessary. Children, on the other hand, know that if a crisis occurs they will be the ones having to make decisions.

A compelling reason for discussions that address future possibilities is that parents may lose their capacities suddenly, plunging the whole family into a crisis. Just when all are least able to think clearly, children may have to make a life-changing decision on behalf of their parents. That decision is more likely to be acceptable if parents have talked about what they would prefer should such an event occur. There is no guarantee that these wishes will be met because no one can predict available resources or the health needs that the emergency brings, but at least, parents will have made their desires known. Children want what they think the best for their parents. Talk ahead of time leaves everyone better able to deal with the necessity of a new decision.

Old age and its failings can be a demanding time of life for both parents and children. Despite everyone's best intentions, stress can and does occur. There will be times, perhaps many of them, when there is a gap between a parent's practical and emotional needs and the children's physical and emotional capacities. The two sides of this equation are constantly changing and are not always equal. That this is a formula for potential misunderstanding and resentment is unsurprising.

Most families make and adjust to the necessary changes with grace. But to pretend that it is always easy is to deny reality. It will be hard for everyone. Facing that there are some things you can no longer do for yourself, you have to accommodate to others' ways of doing. Your children have to juggle the demands on them so that they can help you. Each of you, parent or child, has the capacity to make this new situation better or worse. Some friction is probably unavoidable, but honesty, good humor and an understanding of each other will help. For parents, it is worth considering the paradox that you are more able to maintain your coveted sense of independence if you accept aid when you need it. Independence does not require an obstinate refusal to use assistance. I have talked with many distraught children whose parents long to remain in their own homes but refuse the services that would make that possible.

I do not know that we grow wiser as we age, but if we can do anything to plan for our old age, accept help and change when necessary, then we have a measure of wisdom.

WHAT DO YOU WANT, AND NOT WANT FROM YOUR CHILDREN?

The answer to this question will vary with your age, and, more significantly, with your health. While healthy, you gave as much, perhaps more, to your children as they to you. But the ratio usually changes as you become less mobile and strong. Looking ahead, you have probably said, and meant it, that your fervent hope is that your children will care about you but never for you. But, the realities of old age have a way of outdating earlier intentions. When you are in need, those who love you find that caring about is inseparable from caring for.

As you begin to need help, you may find it worthwhile to ask yourself what you expect from your children. Don't be quick to answer, "Nothing." Deep down, you probably have some expectations, though you may not realize it until you feel upset about something you child has, or has not, done. One client complained to me that none of her six children seemed to notice that since their father fell sick she was worn out by caring for him. They all phoned frequently, one sent flowers regularly, and another had visited recently. As she talked, she recognized that she was expecting them all to visit on a regular basis. And yet, she reflected, two of them lived across the country, another's wife had a disability and could not be left alone, and another's young son had a severe illness. In her distress she had expected something that was not realistic. She continued to feel physically overextended, but at least her feelings were not hurt by her perception that her family was uncaring.

So what are your expectations? Perhaps you secretly think that your children owe it to you to help with everything that you can no longer do for yourself. That if they loved you they would visit more often or call more frequently. Do you think that your children should know what you want without you telling them? So often we expect those we love to read our minds. "But its not worth much if I have to ask," we say, making the mistake of confusing love with clairvoyance. If we assume that others should be so intuitive that they know what we want without guidance we help create confusion and frustration. Are you being realistic, or even, fair?

Getting the assistance you need is a two-way process that involves you as well as your family. As parents you have to learn what your children are willing and able to do. Not what you wish, or think, they should do, but what as individuals is within their capacities. You need to let your children know how to help you. Left to their own observations, they may see you as more independent than you feel, or, conversely, decide that they should take over. Do you want them to take the initiative when they see something they think is wrong, or would you prefer to stay in charge and for them not to act unilaterally? Without guidance, children can only guess whether their parents will welcome their intervention or will regard it as intrusive, where their parents will feel relieved or will feel diminished.

Your children's capacities are limited—by their abilities, their responsibilities, their personalities, where they live. And your children differ from each other, varying in their strengths, their relationship with you, their own personal situations. Or, you may have only one child or none that can be of support.

As you look at these variables in your family, you may realize that you and your children have already worked out some expectations of each other. "Expectation" may be too strong a word for what is an informal system of reliance. Everyone knows who is usually able and willing to help with particular tasks. A child who lives nearby can be depended on for help in emergencies, another to visit every few weeks and to take on odd jobs, one to deal with money matters, and so on. At its best, it is a system that is able to accommodate more or less to everybody's needs and availability.

As clients talk to me about their adult children, I am often struck by what a complex process providing help is. Working out what needs to be done, and how, can be challenging enough; but it's simple compared with being sensitive to others' feelings. When we can no longer do something for ourselves, it takes little to make most of us feel useless and incompetent.

Children are in a complicated place too, especially if their parent is quite infirm and unable to make decisions or care for him- or herself. Such a situation requires much sensitivity. There is a much used phrase "parenting a parent," which is misguided and unhelpful in it's implication that very infirm people are like children. Not so. However diminished, parents are embarrassed by needing help with basic tasks such as showering. If they are also treated or spoken to as if they were young children their dignity will be further threatened.

The inherent conflict in some situations was made obvious to me recently when, in one week, two of my clients were preparing to move out of their homes into an assisted living facility. In both cases, their children were packing up their belongings before moving them. While both women were appreciative of the help, they were also uncharacteristically irritable and critical. One of them summed up her feelings: "They're so competent that my self esteem is just draining away." The other rankled against the lack of consultation. "They move so fast. I don't know where anything is." Both needed things to go more slowly so that they could retain some sense of control. But their children had needs too, and needs that were in conflict with those of their mothers. They had to complete the move, see their mothers settled, and return to their families and jobs by Monday.

Do tasks like this have to end with everyone feeling debilitated and annoyed—at least temporarily? The answer is, "Sometimes, yes." It may be impossible to combine efficiency with sufficient understanding and patience. But the verbal recognition that the situation is hard for the other is amazingly powerful at easing any tension. "This must be hard for you, Mom," or "Thanks so much for doing this for me. I know you're busy," sound simple and obvious. But sometimes it's easy to forget to say it.

Many of your problems can be helped, but not in the way you wish. One of the challenging aspects of being on the receiving end of help is that others never do things quite as you are used to. If flexibility were a prerequisite of old age life would certainly be easier for everyone. It is understandable that you prefer someone in the family to stay with your disabled spouse when necessary, or to take you shopping when you can no longer drive but circumstances may be such that you have to compromise and get help in another way. My brother is willing to help my mother with many tasks, but he does balk at mowing her grass. He would prefer to find someone to do that job so that he can spend his visits on activities where he is more indispensable, such as managing her finances or taking her out for lunch.

More painfully, there are some problems that have no solution. Practical difficulties are easy compared with problems of the heart. Old age brings many losses for which there is no replacement. However attentive your family, they cannot make all well. Certainly, no one can wipe away the loneliness you feel after your spouse or a lifelong friend has died. It helps to talk to someone who is a good listener, but grief and loneliness are for a particular person and no one can take that pain away.

Many times, children and parents will not behave exactly as the other would like. Nor are their responses always what the other wants to hear. If you are disappointed in the response you get, you can be upset or you can try to be sympathetic to other's situation. With compassion both parties may move closer to an understanding of each other. Whatever happens do not make the mistake of interpreting another's shortcomings as lack of love. Always try to appreciate that your parent or your children are probably doing the best they can.

TALK TO EACH OTHER

I am about to return to one of my themes. When things begin to fall apart, it is especially important that you talk to each other. I am amazed by how frequently parents and children, even those who are emotionally close, fail to talk forthrightly. Parents may withhold information from their children, telling themselves that their children are "too busy" or "have enough to worry about." Meanwhile, their children may hesitate to ask important questions or assume that they know the answers. Armed with incomplete data, each guesses at what the other needs or wants. One of my clients told me that she felt neglected by her children. She has disabling, but not life-threatening, health problems; and when the pain is intense she feels lonely and afraid. Because she presents herself to her children as she always has, as a strong, capable and independent woman, she does not tell them how desolate she sometimes feels. So, she's angry and hurt at their lack of attention and they are alienated and confused by her irritable moods.

Like my friend, many older people hate to acknowledge that they need help, and see it as a form of weakness or proof of their decline. Grown up in a society and generation that valued self reliance, they were taught to keep their troubles to themselves. Adult children, however, are more comfortable talking about their feelings and can be frustrated by the "stiff upper lip" approach of their parents. If you are someone who hesitates to talk about your worries, fears or pleasures, you might experiment with someone you trust. You may find that you feel less burdened and that the relationship becomes more intimate.

As your circumstances change, so will your state of mind. When feeling well, all of us can handle more than when we are sick or overwhelmed; and for old people even minor illnesses can markedly affect their mood and ability to cope with everyday matters. Another thing that happens to most of us when we are ill or troubled is that we become rather self-centered. Stress never improved anyone's disposition. We focus on ourselves, seeing others' actions only as they impact us. One of my clients sounded bitter when she told me that her daughter was visiting. "But she's only staying two days. I don't know why she bothers to come." My client had lost sight of her daughter as someone with a job and family, and was in danger of creating a tension filled visit.

One of the most helpful things we can do for our children is to care about them and show it. At difficult times, our talk may be one-sided and full of our troubles. We forget to show interest in our children's lives. If that becomes the norm, our conversations will be boring and dispiriting for everyone. It may be worth asking ourselves occasionally what we are like to talk to or visit? If you suspect that you are often negative and complaining, or that you rarely ask about others' lives, it is time to do something about it. Your time with friends and family can be more pleasurable than that.

With all these changes and fluctuations, it is inevitable that none of us is capable of reading another's mind all or even most of the time. One of the frustrations for children is that most parents want help on their terms—where and how they perceive they need it. Meanwhile children define their parents' problems and the solutions from their own point of view. To improve our communication, there is only one answer. We must all try to talk honestly and to learn about each other by asking questions and then listening to the answers. The challenge, and it is an important one, is not necessarily to agree, but to understand each others' point of view. To achieve that, you all have to listen attentively and keep your mind open, even to suggestions you are tempted to dismiss out of hand. Make suggestions of your own. In any discussion it is easier to find fault with other's ideas but much more constructive to stay with the positive, stressing what you would like and think is possible. Wanting things to return to the way they were, though understandable, is not a productive place to put much energy. All this is a tall order, I know. But it is a vital process to attempt.

Despite everyone's best efforts, there will be many times when advice outnumbers thoughtful questions or observations. Eager to solve perceived problems, most people prefer to generate possible solutions, and that is the way they try to be helpful. You will often fail to find suggestions as welcome and obviously helpful as the speaker believes. I have heard many adult children resolve that they will not be resistant to every idea as they find their parents to be. When their turn comes their children will probably have similar complaints. While there is every reason why no one should unthinkingly accept another's idea, there are also many reasons why those coming from people who know you well should be seriously considered. If tempted to brush a suggestion aside, or say, "No, it won't work," try to delay stating your opinion, and instead, give it some thought. You'll probably need time to get used to the idea, to view it from

all angles, and then make up your mind. Should you decide against it, your relatives will be more likely to let the
matter drop if you explain your reasons, even if they disagree with you.

One of my clients had to have help after her husband
had a stroke. She was determined to care for him at home.
Her children, who lived some distance away, went into action on the telephone. They lined up visiting nurses and
health aides and began to search for a caregiver so that their
mother could go out occasionally. She refused every suggestion. Though nurse's visits seemed necessary for her husband, she was always on the verge of cancelling even them.
"I never know when she's coming." "We don't like people in
our house all the time."

When I met with the whole family, she and her children were able to air and hear each others' concerns. My
client's life had been drastically changed by her husband's illness, and now she felt pushed to accept all kinds of services
that she barely understood and certainly did not like. Her
children, meanwhile, heard her growing more impatient
and irritable, and could not understand why she did not
use the available help, which was designed to make her life
easier. At the meeting, though, they were able to recognize
that their mother was being pressed to accept too much in
too short a time. Some of their suggestions would have to
wait. For her part, my client agreed that the nurse was essential. She would have a health aide to help her husband
with a shower and not threaten to dismiss her before an
agreed trial period. The door was left open for other services
to be reconsidered in the future.

Some children deal with their anxieties by becoming autocratic, by giving much advice too often and forcefully. If you suspect that your parents feel overly managed or harassed by a flood of instructions, check with them. They probably appreciate your concern, but might like you to ease off so that they can think about what you have said. Their sense of well-being usually depends on doing as much for themselves as possible. Your interest and support are vital, but taking over where they are capable is not. Listen to your parents as you would like them to listen to you; namely with respect and an open mind. An elderly friend was constantly urged by her daughter and neighbors to have help with her housework. "What would I do? Sit and watch them do my cleaning?" she said. I thought she was wise. Her determination to care for herself kept her mobile and gave meaning to her life.

Finally, do not hesitate to communicate that you appreciate each other. It is important for you all to know that you make a positive difference. It is helpful to be specific. "I really enjoyed that ride." "I really appreciate that I can depend on you when I need help." "I admire that with all you are going through you always ask how my life is." It is a mistake to assume that children and parents know that they are valued for who they are and what they do. Maybe they do not know. If they do know, they will enjoy hearing it again. Thanks is like love in that we thrive on hearing the words as often as they are felt.

POINTS TO CONSIDER

- As old age and infirmity arrive most people have to depend on others to meet some of their needs. Seeing their parents fail, children too will enter a new stage of their lives.

- Tensions may occur as parents feel managed and diminished by their children's suggestions, while children are frustrated by their parents' resistance to help. Listen to one another and try to stress what is acceptable and possible. Give each other time to get used to a new situation, and recognize that returning to the past is not a viable choice.

- Of course we cannot know what the future holds but it is worth exploring where and how you want to be cared for—should you need it—before a crisis occurs. Make your children part of the discussion.

- A parent's decline is hard for everyone. Try to understand what others are going through.

- Be open with each other. If you try to guess what the other is thinking you may be wrong.

- Remember to express love for, and appreciation of, each other.

- Show an interest in each other's lives. Even when things begin to fall apart, conversations can be interesting and enjoyable.

Special Problems

In general, I write as if children grow into more or less self-sufficient adults, able to care for themselves and for others. We may complain that our children still need a financial handout occasionally or that they call about every emotional up and down of their lives, but for the most part they mature enough to become independent of us. That is not always so, however. For a variety of reasons—developmental handicap, accident, physical or mental illness—some children have to cope with limitations not handed out to most of us and, even as adults, need considerable help in order to manage their lives. They may lack the capacity to hold a job, develop friendships, handle money, or care for themselves. Usually their chief resource, their parents have responsibilities and concerns that extend not only beyond the legal end of parental duty, but sometimes for the rest of their own lives.

A different type of concern that many families have to confront is substance abuse. All of us, at any age, can fall into the trap of misusing drugs or alcohol. While family members watch helplessly, the effects of abuse may spread, damaging marriages, children, health and trust in its wake.

This chapter addresses problems that are not faced by all families but when they occur they are accompanied by special struggles and heartaches.

CHILDREN WITH DISABILITIES

Each disability carries its own limitations, grief and challenges. Your child's condition may have been obvious since birth, or perhaps occurred in adolescence or early adulthood. It may affect mobility, speech, learning or behavior. It may be evident to anyone seeing him or her, or only be noticeable under certain circumstances. You alone know what particular problems you and your child have to face. And you know that though challenges evolve as the years pass, most do not disappear.

Although all parents worry about their children at times, those who have a child with special needs have more to be concerned about. Not only may their child be more difficult to raise, but their environment is often inadequate to meet their needs, and even unwelcoming. I remember hearing the mother of a young child being criticized for being overprotective. As I knew that her son had poor eyesight and hearing I wondered how many of us would choose not to take extra precautions if in that mother's situation. Insensitive remarks, gratuitous advice and looks of disapproval just add to the stress of parents like this mother.

Faced with difficulties out of the ordinary, parents often have to learn to be experts in their child's condition, and then to become advocates to ensure that necessary help is provided. Most parents I know who have young children with special needs are pushed into being more assertive than is comfortable for them as they strive to obtain the educational and health services their children require.

These parents' lives are different in ways they could never have foreseen. Their hopes not only for their children but also for themselves have to be modified. The expectation that their children will become self-sufficient may not be realized, nor their own retirement plans for leisure and travel. They and their handicapped child may be stuck with each other long after most children leave home. Neither parent nor child chooses dependency, but there often appears to be no acceptable and available alternative.

However compromised in their ability to function without assistance, all children long to be like everyone else of their age. A dependency that is acceptable at 10 years, even 17, becomes painful by adulthood. Your son or daughter may not be able to cope with the world without help but he or she will almost certainly want to do so. Herein lie some of the many challenges for the parents. How to provide the necessary aid while continuing to build their children's self-esteem? How to recognize their children's needs but also their aspirations as adults? How to help them be as independent as they can be?

I remember a mother of a little girl with cerebral palsy who attended a clinic where I worked. She was articulate about how difficult it was to decide when her daughter needed help, and when to let her try to manage on her own. Parents of all young children will do anything to protect their offspring from danger and hurt, but gradually restrain their natural instincts so that the youngsters learn to make their own wise decisions. For parents with an unusually vulnerable child these choices are harder to make. This mother said that every instinct in her insisted that she must stay near her daughter to protect her at all times. When the teacher encouraged her to drop the little girl off at preschool without drawing out her goodbyes, the mother felt that she must be present to interpret her child's needs to the other children and staff. With time and reassurance the mother was able to see for herself that her daughter was coping well without her on hand at all times.

The urge to protect does not end with childhood. Though your adult children may need help in many areas of living, sooner or later they resist living under the roof and control of their parents. Though tempting to keep your child at home where you know he is safe and well cared for, in reality, most adult children, disabled or not, do better living away from home, returning home only for visits. They feel better about themselves—more competent and confident. Understandably, many parents are unwilling to let their adult children live in sheltered or group housing under the care of professionals. They are frightened for their children and sometimes reluctant to recognize their limitations. "He doesn't need a place with people like that," they may think. In their anxiety they may be unable to see that their child is ready to leave home and that there comes a time when most of us benefit from guidance and supervision from people other than our parents.

There is nothing quite like paid work for helping people to feel worthwhile. Depending on your children's abilities they may need help with certain aspects of a job. They may benefit from extra supervision, do better in a quiet, calm atmosphere, or prefer tasks that have a clear routine. Again, vocational services and specialized organizations for the disabled are a resource. If work can be part of life for your children, they will expand socially and in self-assurance.

Former clients of mine have a seriously developmentally delayed son. They were afraid that if he went to a residential program, as had been suggested by social workers, his behavior would regress. For many years they cared for him at home. Eventually as he grew into middle age and their health deteriorated, he became too difficult for them to handle. He now lives in a group home, coming home at weekends. He is no longer angry, they are more relaxed and all are able to have some good times. Despite their earlier misgivings they now believe he is much happier—and so are they.

Parents who have a child needing special help usually have other children to care for also. However aware the parents are of all their children's needs, there is rarely enough time and energy to go around. A child with a disability may have hospital stays, a long list of exercises to be done daily and supervised by a parent, frequent therapy appointments; the list goes on. Professionals with the best of intentions do not always remember that their recommendations may be too many for the over-extended parents to carry out.

Despite their parents' efforts, siblings of children with special needs almost certainly receive less than their share of parental attention. Since each situation, child and family is different, some children may suffer and have to face their own problems, whereas others may become especially caring and sensitive human beings. Parents who are open about the problems faced by their disabled child, do not burden their other children with child care but encourage them to be involved siblings, are more likely to foster empathy and thoughtfulness in the whole family.

MENTAL ILLNESS

Some mental illnesses are so severe that its victims cannot hold a job or even live independently. Schizophrenia, bi-polar illness and borderline personality are conditions that may threaten the ability to lead a normal life. Symptoms and their severity vary from patient to patient. Diagnosis is often not easy, as many parents find to their frustration, and treatment may go through several trials before a good fit is found. Like parents of all disabled children, those with serious mental illness usually have to provide support, advocacy and emotional energy for the rest of their lives.

One of the tragedies and difficulties of the serious mental illnesses is how it affects a person's behavior: it appears to define who he or she is. Someone with schizophrenia may have fixed delusions, making much conversation one-tracked and even senseless to most listeners. Bi-polar illness causes moods that swing between depression and mania and may be severe enough that a sense of reality is lost. Those with Borderline Personality Disorder experience intense emotions and unpredictable behavior that bewilder and frighten everyone involved. For families, these conditions bring anguish and confusion as they try to make sense of their relative's behavior.

There are medications that help with the management of all these illnesses but there is no guarantee that patients will take their meds as prescribed. Often unaware that anything is wrong with them, people suffering from these conditions see no reason for taking something that may have unpleasant side effects. Or, they begin to do better and decide they need no more treatment. These illnesses are not curable, and can only be ameliorated by treatment. Medications usually have to be taken for life. They are helpful—sometimes very helpful—but unfortunately do not have the power to cure.

It is not possible to force someone to comply with treatment. You may know that your child has fewer symptoms and is easier to live with when he takes his medication but he has no perspective on that. It often takes years of suffering for patients and their families before a patient accepts his illness and the need for consistent treatment.

Nor does a patient have any control over her symptoms. Telling a sick person to "pull up your socks" or "calm down" is not only useless but may reinforce any sense of self-blame that she feels already.

What you can do is to be as supportive, open and honest as possible. If your child's mood is volatile try to stay calm and low-key emotionally. Many sick people feel more secure if routines and surroundings are predictable.

Should your child be abusive you must set some limits. You must protect yourself and your family from emotional or physical harm. In extreme instances, you may have to call the police.

I had a client whose middle-aged daughter had never been able to create any stability for herself. She had no relationships, no job, and no peace. She called her mother frequently and at great length. Every conversation quickly deteriorated into abuse, mostly directed at her mother for being an inadequate, uncaring parent. My client had been beaten down by her daughter's angry criticism to the point that she believed it. Her guilt prevented her from putting the phone down and thus ending the stream of invective.

Despite the mother's attempts at peace-making the long conversations were worse than useless. The daughter became increasingly loud and hostile while her mother felt even more despairing and critical of herself. Warning her daughter that she would not listen to such unpleasantness, and then acting on her words, would at least have started a habit of useful limit-setting.

SUBSTANCE ABUSE

Addiction to drugs, prescribed or otherwise, and alcohol can occur at any age; it can also be treated at any age. Although substance abuse is a problem widely associated with young men it is also common in women and the elderly. It can wreak havoc in any home—humble or grand, rich or poor.

Many abusers are so effectively secretive about their habit that few people outside the immediate family, except drinking buddies, are aware of what is going on. If you do notice that a relative has a problem with alcohol or drugs, choose a private time and state your concerns calmly, but seriously. Since denial is a notorious feature of substance abuse your relative will, in all likelihood, minimize how often and how much he or she drinks or attribute it to stress, depression, or other factors. By all means express your love and your hope that he or she will take steps to end this damaging habit, but know that addiction is an extremely difficult habit to break. You may think that your words have been useless but it is possible that your concern may be remembered and bear fruit later.

Most abusers do not seek treatment, until they 'hit bottom', by losing an important relationship or their job. This is so excruciating to watch that you might find yourself making excuses for your relative or agreeing with their own explanations. You will only prolong the situation. Before you can be in a position to be helpful you must be clear in your own mind that no one can take the first step except the addicted family member.

By all means learn about substance use and consider talking to a substance abuse counselor about suggestions he or she might have. Professional guidance is important. Most abusers are typically resistant to the idea of needing help and unlikely to listen to suggestions coming from a family member. There are some treatment methods available—counseling, medication, family meetings, intensive treatment centers and, above all, Alcoholics Anonymous—but a professional is an essential member of the team. Most people need professional help; will power is rarely strong enough.

An invaluable resource for families and friends of an alcoholic is Al-Anon. There you can learn what approaches may be, and may not, be useful.

ELDERLY SUBSTANCE ABUSE

In the elderly, substance abuse is largely hidden, often unrecognized and rarely addressed. For the most part it occurs in the home and goes unnoticed except by the family.

People who have been drinking heavily and regularly for decades, with no apparent ill effects on their behavior, may in their old age become affected by smaller amounts of alcohol. For instance, they may become confused, uncertain of their balance, garrulous or irritable after one or two drinks, and not believe that anything is amiss. As bodies age, their ability to metabolize alcohol deteriorates, and so one drink has a much greater effect than in the past.

There are certain events common in old age that may put some people at risk for using alcohol more than they have in the past. Almost without noticing it, those suffering from chronic pain, grief, loneliness and isolation may try to dull their pain by reaching for alcohol or pills.

In addition to alcohol, medications are the most commonly misused by this age group. Like alcohol, many medications have a stronger effect on the bodies of elderly people and so produce negative effects, compounding the problem for which the pill was taken. A further complication is that elderly people often take many medicines, sometimes prescribed by different doctors for a variety of physical conditions. The combination may produce more side-effects than any one pill would alone. If an elderly person becomes suddenly confused or lethargic, medication may be the culprit.

Medications bought over the counter are also subject to abuse and misuse. Many people assume that because they are easy to obtain they are harmless and can be taken freely. "Three pills must be better than two" is a risky supposition.

If your spouse or your children express concern about your use of alcohol or medicines, take them seriously. Try not to get defensive. Instead, ask what they have observed. If the discussion becomes unpleasant, you can end it but try to remember what they said and return to the subject at a calmer time.

I had a client who quit a lifetime of heavy drinking at the age of 79 years. What motivated him was that his grandchildren had become reluctant to visit him. He was grateful to Alcoholics Anonymous for the remaining 10 years of his life, not only for providing guidance and support but also a group of friends. What delighted him most was that his children and grandchildren were so proud of him.

"WHAT WILL HAPPEN WHEN WE DIE?"

This is a major question for those of you whose children need lifelong help, and it needs attention before you become infirm. If your child is connected to an appropriate social agency, talk to the professionals about possible resources; if not, make that connection as soon as possible. You will be doing your child a service if you plan and even arrange a move for him or her while you are still available to provide love and support. You can hope and even expect that your other children will keep in touch but you cannot assume they will take your place. No one can give your disabled child the love and dedication that you do, but there is loving and respectful care available.

Parenting is a challenging job at the best of times. All parents want the same for their children; for them to live contented and fulfilled lives. When disability occurs, however, parenting presents extraordinary dilemmas. At times your child's limitations may be painfully evident, especially when he is with peers, or involved with the medical or school system. As for all your children you have to accept that the specifics of a fulfilling life do not have to include everything that is important to you. Academic achievement, marriage, children, and financial success are not prerequisites of a happy life. Giving and receiving love and kindness, and a sense of self-worth are more important attributes and within reach of us all. What is also true is that pride and pleasure in your children often comes in unexpected places.

Being a parent of a child with special problems can be lonely. Whatever the challenges you face, you probably receive too much advice, well-intentioned but usually unwelcome. You may find that the stigma attached to some illnesses encourages you to keep your struggles to yourself. Most of us, though, do need to open our hearts to a good listener on occasion.

There are excellent support groups for family members. Al-Anon, A.M.I. (Association for the Mentally Ill) and "special needs" services, provided by state or voluntary organizations, exist in most parts of the country. There you will find people who understand what you are going through and are happy to share what they have learned and found useful. In time you will give the same support to others. Contrary to what many imagine there is plenty of laughter in most support groups. It is the therapeutic humor of recognition and compassion.

POINTS TO CONSIDER

- Whatever your child's disability, help him be as independent and like others of his age as is possible.
- All parents have to let go of some of their dreams for their children, and you may have to let go of more than

most, but there are many successes and occasions for pride.

- People with a serious mental illness usually do better in an orderly and predictable environment. Though it is often difficult, try to keep your own emotions at a calm level. It is essential that those with a mental illness take their medications consistently.

- Abuse of alcohol, drugs and medications affects many families. As the victims are invariably resistant to changing their behavior, it is important to enroll the help of a substance abuse counselor.

- If your child is abusive under any circumstances you must set limits to protect yourself and your family.

- Whatever you do, look into the services offered by your state and non-profit organizations. Here are some widely available resources. These services exist to help you and your child receive the aid you need.

  a. Developmental Disabilities Council

  b. Mental Health Centers

  c. Associations for specific conditions, e.g. cerebral palsy, the blind, the deaf.

  d. National Association on Mental Illness

  e. Alcoholics Anonymous, Al-anon, Narcotics Anonymous.

Differences and Reconciliation

How wonderful it would be if we could all—parents, children, siblings, and grandchildren—have a happy relationship with each other. The reality is that we get on less well with certain family members than we would like. With some we have little in common, others we find boringly self-centered, and a particular child seems disruptive and demanding. Such minor irritations are part of life and we can handle them for the relatively infrequent times we spend together. But what about conflict serious enough that a certain member refuses to attend family events, that a child or sibling has been estranged for years, that a daughter-in-law never visits if she can avoid it, or a son rejects any invitation where his brother might be present? Such rifts cast a cloud over any gathering. The absent person is the elephant in the room—someone whose absence everyone notices but no one wants to talk about for fear of upsetting others. In every sense except physical that person is present and everyone else feels uncomfortable.

A separation caused by enmity becomes more entrenched and more difficult to mend as time passes. On a recent visit my mother was talking about her only surviving sister with whom she has had no contact for many years. She and Mary had never been close even as children but my mother dates the rift from a family funeral when apparently Mary was rude to her. (As so often happens with long lasting quarrels the details have been lost over the years though the feelings have not.) The first upset was followed by other incidents when Mary, in my mother's opinion, ignored her or treated her unpleasantly. In response to my surprise at the survival of this acrimonious feeling between them, my mother said that she would make no more efforts towards her sister for fear of being hurt again. "It is easier to ignore her," she said. But the heightened emotion in her voice told me that ease was a state of mind she has not achieved.

Since the two sisters are in their 90s and do not live near each other it seems unlikely that this relationship will ever be anything but negative. It probably had its seeds in the inevitable jealousies and favoritism among the eight children in their family. Could my mother or Mary have made a positive move towards the other, and would either have responded in kind? I will never know. But, given the circumstances it seems unlikely to happen now. And does it matter since they were never close anyway? Personally, I think it does. My mother's blood pressure rises when she thinks about Mary. Mary's son takes obvious care not to mention her on his visits to my mother. It is fair to assume that this friction brings discomfort to several people.

A characteristic of anger and resentment is that they hurt us, the owner, more than anyone else. Negative emotions take up much energy and psychic space, leaving less room for happier feelings. Like my mother you may think that you no longer care about the person who has hurt you, but if you feel anger or sorrow whenever his or her name is mentioned, you do care and are spending emotional energy in a way that is harmful to you.

Our feelings about each other are colored by our shared past. History is a powerful force in families. Even when children share the same parents the experience of each child is like no other. One child felt unloved, another remembers a happy childhood, and another was unprotected from a bullying sibling.

These emotions do not disappear when children reach adulthood. For most of us any pain fades but under certain circumstances it will be aroused and we find ourselves besieged by old hurts. We long for our father to show us some affection. We hope that our mother will eventually find some reason to praise us.

A friend described her sense of walking on eggshells whenever she met her sister. Her sister had always been jealous of her, and it was easy to unwittingly upset her. Visits were easily spoiled by an incident or remark that would have been insignificant had they been better friends.

A sense of the past may throw some helpful light on the origins of these painful feelings, making them easier to deal with in a constructive manner, but all too often the past is used to justify present resentments that in turn refuel the animosity. Attuned to be angry with a certain person we easily see further reasons for renewed anger, and so the cycle continues. Before long that person can do nothing right.

There are at least two parties in any disagreement, each being upset with the other and feeling justified in his or her feelings. The truth is that there is no such thing as a pure right or a pure wrong. Life is more complicated than that.

When we are mad, though, it is almost impossible to see the other's point of view. All we see is our own. Without a broader vision we are immersed in conflict.

Human interactions are so complex and multifaceted that it is perhaps surprising that most of us get on as well with our families as we do. Fortunately, the bonds of kinship are strong and resilient enough to withstand most shocks and bad weather. Should they weaken there are social and personal forces to push us back together, reminding us that there are more important matters in life than winning every disagreement. Blood ties, tradition of family cohesion, pressure from other members of the family all work towards healing any rift.

Clients of mine who had always thought they were close to their children were taken totally unawares when their college age daughter announced that she and her boy friend, whom they had met only once, had got married. They felt betrayed, angry and embarrassed. After some weeks of painful discussion and explanations they all decided that their relationship was too important to sacrifice it because of a quarrel. That the couple had chosen to marry away from the family remained hurtful but taking a wide view, not serious enough for a rupture.

ESTRANGED CHILDREN
Although all family rifts are uncomfortable, the most painful are those between parents and their children. Many parents and their children have disagreements with each other, fail to be good friends and even visit rarely, but nevertheless most do expect to be important to each other for

as long as they live. When that expectation is shattered because affection and interest have faded, everyone involved has no doubt that much is seriously amiss. For parents especially sorrow is deep and abiding, and from what I have seen is usually accompanied by a sense of guilt and shame. "Where did we go wrong?" It is a question for which they rarely have a good answer. Nor do children cut off relations with their parents willingly. They must have strong reasons for feeling that separation is the only solution for them at present.

Most parents are only too aware that they are not, and never have been, perfect. We are all sorry about our failure to be patient, our absence of foresight, or that our paid job took up so much time away from the family. No one, including our children, grows through childhood scot-free. Parents cannot meet all their children's needs or protect them from every hurt and danger. Teenage years are almost inevitably marked by tension, when parents and children have to bear much criticism. For most, this is a stage that passes, and by adulthood, children, sometimes to their surprise, find that they have much in common with their parents. They gradually see their parents not as a handicap, but as human beings, flawed as are we all, but people for whom they have affection.

If children or parents carry their hurts and disappointments into the children's adult years their relationship will be tense and unsatisfying. At worst there will be a complete rift, at best an uneasy truce that erupts periodically into unpleasantness.

MOVING TOWARD RECONCILIATION

Fortunately there is always reason to hope that some effort on your part may improve a relationship. Depending on personalities and circumstances the changes might be small and proceed at snail's pace, but an important consideration is that even minor changes can be significant.

If you can, make a friendly move soon after a quarrel has occurred. It is probably wise to allow time for you and your family member to settle down somewhat, but leaving too much time gives bad feelings the opportunity to harden. Whether you chose to write, phone or meet depends on logistics and your comfort level but, in any case, you have to be ready to give up your need to be right and for the other person to be wrong. If you are not ready, wait until you are.

Make your first message short— something along the line that you are sorry about the unpleasantness that happened, and you hope that he like you is willing to talk about it. You may not receive a reply but do not despair. Follow up with a suggestion that you meet for a walk or lunch. Keep the door open with occasional calls or notes.

A source of distress for one of my elderly clients was the divorce of her son and her inability to see her grandsons who lived with their mother in England. She sent birthday and Christmas cards but never received a reply. She was discouraged but persevered, hoping that as they reached adulthood perhaps they would respond. Then one day she heard from one of her grandsons that he was to attend a US college for a semester and hoped to visit her. She had had a long wait but she was finally rewarded.

If your family member is willing to talk with you, your best approach is to listen as attentively as possible. Criticism, lecturing or crying are not productive. Your goal is to learn what is upsetting her. Many people are not skilled at talking about their feelings—indeed they may not know what they are feeling—but if you can make a habit of listening and asking occasional questions, you will create a supportive and interested atmosphere.

If at any time you realize that you did make a mistake, take responsibility for it and make amends. With a heartfelt and full apology your relationship will already have made a small start towards recovery. Carrying a load of guilt and self-criticism helps no one, but showing compassion and a genuine attempt to understand does. You cannot determine how the other will react but if you keep the focus on how he feels, you will probably mollify any harsh outcome.

Though it is never easy to hear you have pained someone, you can regret that you hurt her. You do not need to accept blame unless you do feel responsible, but you can tell her that you are sorry she is upset. Of course you will long to explain your side, protesting that you loved her just as much as her sister, or recalling that you were dealing with a divorce at the time or grieving a friend's death, but your point of view is not relevant at this moment. What is important is that though your parent's or child's complaints may make little sense to you, they are real and powerful to each of them. That is what you have to accept.

Rifts develop in different ways, some occurring dramatically with an angry quarrel, while others happen slowly as people drift apart until there is no contact at all. For any healing to occur, someone has to make the first move. Here pride is the huge barrier. To approach someone you have quarreled with, and to do so in a conciliatory way, takes courage. Our pride encourages us to maintain our hurt and our sense of righteousness, but that is the most effective way of preventing change. Holding on to your determination to be seen to be right comes at a high price for you and your relationship. It is far better to respectfully agree to differ.

I remember an older woman who had a longstanding distaste for her daughter-in-law. The feeling was clearly mutual because they successfully managed to avoid meeting each other even though they lived in the same town. She came to see me because her son was upset that she had not invited his wife to her husband's memorial service. She felt quite justified because her daughter-in-law never paid her any attention. After a long discussion she said, "I don't care for her manner but nor do I like the way I'm responding. Perhaps I'll tell my son I'll invite her."

What we do with our hurt and anger is our responsibility. Waiting for the other person to make the first move is an unsatisfactory option. And not responding to someone else's opening, however clumsy, similarly lets pride win over grace.

COMPASSION

The most powerful antidote to negative feelings is compassion. By putting ourselves in the shoes of those who hurt us, not as we would wear them, but as they wear them, we can try to see their struggles, deprivations, hopes and despair. Our critical judgment fades as our understanding grows.

While not condoning their action we find their negative behavior at least easier to understand. We may realize that we
all have much in common, and given certain circumstances
we cannot be sure that we would not behave like those we
condemn.

Early in my career as a therapist, I remember being irritated with a client who saw her life as totally negative.
Thinking about her after our first session I realized my
mood came from my frustration at not being able to connect with her. How unhappy she must feel and hopeless
that her life would never change for the better, I thought. As
my annoyance gave way to compassion, we were able to do
some constructive work together.

Compassion cannot be demanded of us but we can
nurture our natural inclination to be kind and thoughtful.
And most of us do want to be kind. As we go about our
daily lives we notice that we can affect the mood of others
by our demeanor and friendliness, or lack thereof. Giving
others our full attention we begin to see who they really are,
and with this clear vision connection becomes possible. We
feel happier and lighter, and others respond positively as
they sense our warmth and interest.

It is also wise to nurture compassion for ourselves. Be-
rating ourselves is only useful if it pushes us to learn from
our mistakes and make amends. Then let our self-criticism
go and focus on the present.

WHEN NOTHING WORKS

Unfortunately, healing does not always occur. Tragically for
those concerned, parents and children, brothers and sisters

may be totally alienated. Sometimes the bonds have been broken by abandonment or abuse, or by a mental illness that has made a positive relationship almost impossible. Whatever the cause, estrangement brings unhappiness and even anguish to all concerned. Even if a family member has made the choice to separate, it is worth remembering that he or she is almost certainly unhappy about it.

Some hurts remain so severe that they retain all their pain. If that is true for you, you may have to accept that in all likelihood you will not have the relationship with your parent, brother, sister or child that you hoped for. Your challenge is to come to terms with your resentment and grief so that the past does not continue to inflict pain on the present.

People come with a range of strengths and weaknesses, and you may be unlucky enough to have a relative with severe inadequacies. Since you cannot rewrite the past you have to reconcile yourself to the limitations of some relationships. Those of us who wait for others to change into what we would like them to be are doomed to disappointment.

A friend had a brother of whom she was never fond. Meanwhile her mother saw no fault in him. After my friend's father died her brother moved in with her mother and gradually appropriated much of her money for his own uses. As in the past, her mother refused to hear any criticism of him. As her mother aged and declined my friend continued to visit her, making sure that she received the help and medical care she needed. When her mother died she chose to have no further contact with her brother.

I remember a young woman in an Alzheimer's support group I was leading. She was one of 12 children and was living with her mother and caring for her. Members of the group expressed surprise that no sibling was giving her significant help. "I am the youngest child and by the time I came along my mother was tired of children," she said. "We never cared for each other much. But now she's no longer herself, I can look after her because she's not the mother who never cared about me but a human being needing care and kindness."

Hearing this young woman's story we would have understood if she had been resentful or at least mired in self-pity. But for some remarkable reason she was able to move beyond carrying a grudge and did what she thought was right. Most of us are not so generous.

When we do harbor negative feelings it is possible to do something about them. Instead of holding on to being a victim and using precious energy ruminating about a bitter past, you can take responsibility for dealing with the situation as wisely as you are able. Sometimes wisdom entails accepting that you can no longer put effort, including anger, into a relationship that no longer means anything to you. Sometimes a relationship is so toxic that you have to stay away for your own sake. Or, like the young woman in the Alzheimer's group, you may choose to step in and do what you can.

Time is running out for us all, and, importantly, we rarely know when it will do so. Imminence of death has a useful way of pointing out matters of significance. Do you want to reach out to your estranged relative one more time? If so, do it now. Does he or she have redeeming qualities? Can you feel any compassion?

If you have proved to your own satisfaction that any further move would be futile, you can work on your own healing. With no action from the person who hurt you, you can recognize that your anger damages you and for your own sake you need to let it go.

A son whose mother was frail came to talk about plans for her care. Their relationship was so acrimonious that he had severed contact with her long ago. Now he was her only close relative and she needed care. His solution was to find her a good nursing home, keep in touch with the staff to ensure she had good care but to have no personal contact. Love had obviously disappeared from this relationship; only duty remained and that was all that the son could fulfill.

Whatever your particular situation you can take responsibility for your own negative feelings. Old hurts cannot be undone or forgotten but they can be detached from emotions that take up energy and cause you distress. You certainly do not have to condone the hurtful behavior nor like the person who perpetrated it. What is important is that you take care of yourself and find more peace of mind.

As a footnote, I want to update the situation between my mother and her sister. My mother has just told me that Mary's son recently called her to say that his mother had been in the hospital for a couple of days—"nothing serious." My mother thought that perhaps he was giving her a hint about reconciling. She immediately sent a "get well" card, and within a few days received a note from Mary. "There're only us two girls left," my mother said, "It's silly not to talk."

In most families members feel some connection with each other. The closer the relationship, the more intense are the feelings for each other, with love, anger and every emotion between usually present. What is not present is indifference. If you have indifference you have nothing. Then there is no connection. Thus with family members it is almost impossible not to care. There is always hope.

POINTS TO CONSIDER

- No one leaves childhood without some emotional damage. Under certain circumstances old hurts arise again and surprise by their persistence and strength.

- A major feature of negative feelings is that the owner usually suffers the most. They use a great deal of energy leaving us fatigued and embittered. There is less room for happier emotions.

- Family relationships are invariably too important to be sacrificed because of a quarrel.

- If you cause someone pain, your task is to listen and try to understand how the other feels. Refrain from explaining your point of view. That is irrelevant at that time.

- If a family member cuts off contact, and you have done what you can to reconnect, try to feel some compassion and remember that he or she has unhappy reasons for the action.

- In any quarrel, pride is a strong impediment to a resolution. You have to give up your need to be right and for the other party to be wrong. If the other does not follow your lead you can at least come to a respectful decision to differ.

- What we do with our own anger and resentment is our responsibility. Waiting for the other to make the first move is not a fruitful option; nor is rejecting another's conciliatory approach, however clumsy.

- Compassion is a powerful healer. If we can put ourselves in another's shoes and appreciate the reasons for his or her negative feelings, our own usually fade leaving us with a more expansive outlook. We can also turn our compassion in our own direction.

- You may be unlucky enough to have a family member with whom, despite your efforts, you cannot have the relationship you would choose. Then you have to settle for what is possible. At worst, you may find someone so toxic that you can have no contact at all. For your own sake, deal with the anger and pain inflicted in the past, so that it does not damage your present.

Wrapping Up

Everyone who reaches an advanced age has already faced many disappointments and successes, joys and sorrows. More challenges lie ahead. Many of them are exclusive to old age, some are not. This is a time for wrapping up your affairs while you are still able to do so. You will need to have discussions with your children because subjects often concern them as much as you. Financial and legal arrangements for your final years, and your wishes for your dying and death are among such topics. When we have died and our children are grieving, we will have helped them a great deal if our affairs are in order and they know what we want.

Other challenges, while not peculiar to old age, are more likely to occur at that stage of life. In particular, there is the need to accept help, the loss of purpose or meaning, and grief. Such emotional hurdles are present at the end of many a life.

ACCEPTING HELP
Most of us dislike being on the receiving end of help especially when it is a necessity rather than a choice. Yet that is a situation we must all confront on occasion. While independence is highly valued in our culture, in reality we swing back and forth between dependence and independence

many times between birth and death. The true state is rather one of interdependence as we both give and receive help throughout our lives. In old age, however, we have less hope that we will ever regain our autonomy—a dispiriting experience. We may feel demoralized, useless, or even a nuisance. Or we may fret that help is never as satisfactory as the care we gave ourselves. The challenge, and it is a difficult one, is to accept our limitations and whatever help is appropriate to our situation. In that way we are able to maintain a sense of self-reliance. Meanwhile, you do not, of course, have to accept help you do not want or need. Where you can rely on yourself by all means do so. But do not let pride cause you to refuse help that could support your independence. Independence is a relative state which people often redefine as they become infirm. A person who receives help with house cleaning, gardening and transport, and is able to stay in her own home feels, and is regarded as, more self-sufficient than someone who rejects help and so has to move to assisted living accommodation.

As I write this I am aware how fraught this issue of help is for many families. In my own family, my siblings and I, and our mother do not often agree on this subject. Some of us think my mother should have help in her house, most of us would like to have more access to her physician, and all of us would like her to appreciate and accept our advice. We have to admit, however, that our mother's determination to look after herself has much wisdom. Housework keeps her physically active, and managing many of her own affairs gives her the comfort of having some control. The reality is that children cannot force their parents, assuming they are cognitively competent, to go against their will. Rather than nag, children do better to keep an eye on how their parents are doing and offer appropriate suggestions as they see the need.

Ironically, we are happy to help others but resist allowing others to do the same for us. One problem may be that as infirmities increase, we do not see that we can return the help we receive. But does that really matter? We know that we have felt good about giving a hand to others and that the expectation of any return was no part of it. So it is for the people who offer to help us. Furthermore, there are many ways of giving that are still available to those of us who are physically infirm. We can be appreciative, be a good friend, and be an example for those who come behind us. Above all, we can help others feel good by receiving their gifts with grace.

GRIEF

Losses come thick and fast in old age. Most painful are the deaths of spouse, family and friends, but the loss of a home, a pet, eyesight or hearing can also be hard to bear. The capacity to love is one of our most human attributes. Like most mental states, though, love has a flip side—grief. We cannot have one without the other, nor would we choose to have no love in our lives.

There is no single pattern to grief. Some mourners are quiet, sharing their feelings only with those closest to them, while others are expressive. Some quickly put their grief behind them as they face the challenges of creating a new life, whereas others openly mourn for the rest of their days. Still others have a delayed reaction, with the deepest sadness coming months after their loved one's death.

Not only does each person feel loss in his or her own way, but also each loss is felt differently. Many circumstances affect your mourning. Was the death sudden or at the end of a long illness? What about your personality? Do you keep your pain to yourself, or do you turn to family and friends for support? What other deaths have you experienced? Often, sadness about an earlier death will rise anew when you experience another loss. What is the meaning of this particular death? What was your relationship like? What did that person mean to you? Ironically, grief may be more painful and prolonged when the relationship was troubled. Regrets and resentments can complicate your mourning whereas in fulfilling relationships the pain, while severe, is eventually eased by happy memories.

Grief is not only for people, of course. A pet's death may be devastating especially for someone who lives alone and has now lost her closest companion. Some older people grieve when they have to move from a home that is intimately associated with a deceased spouse and happy memories.

When a family member dies, your children too will grieve in their way, and the nature of their loss will be different from yours and from each other's. In a time of extreme grief, you are probably so numb that it is difficult to think of others and to appreciate that they may react very differently from you. For instance, if your father has just died you may be angry if a sibling who has rarely visited him, appears at the funeral acting like the chief mourner.

Since all of you will be more sensitive and vulnerable than usual this is not the time for outspoken judgment, but rather for support, patience and kindness.

The loss of a spouse is almost always disorienting, bringing disruption to all aspects of your life. Not only do you lose the companion with whom you have shared your life for many years but also your social partner and the person around whom you have built your daily routine. You probably feel physically unwell, mentally disorganized, emotionally devastated and lost. It will take time to feel like yourself again—certainly a year, maybe several. Your sense of being will gradually improve, so if possible defer life-changing plans until your emotional distress has abated and you can make a balanced decision. I have seen more than one older woman, frightened and lonely after the death of her husband, move in with her children, only for everyone to discover later that it was a poor idea.

As in other troubled times you will probably be given much advice about how to handle your grief. "You'll feel better when the first year is over." Maybe you will, maybe not. "You have to get on with your life." Perhaps all you can do at present is to get through the day. To believe anyone's advice is to risk feeling inadequate. "I can't even do grief right," one client said to me. The truth is that there is no right, wrong or even best way to mourn.

Though you may sense that the best of life has passed, we humans seem mostly programmed to choose life. You will probably regain your capacity for pleasure, gradually picking up the threads of your life. Should your feelings of despair and hopelessness continue with no relief, however, it is important to seek professional help. Your feelings have nothing to do with lack of strength or will power, but everything to do with an extraordinary disruption in every aspect of your being. Counseling, with or without medication, usually brings considerable relief.

LOSS OF MEANING

With children grown, spouse and friends deceased and health deteriorating many old people feel that they have little to live for. "What use am I?" they may ask. Like all of us, the elderly want to feel important to someone and that they have something to contribute. Only too often they feel invisible and superfluous.

It is largely within the context of their families that most of the very old find meaning. Many aspects of life that gave purpose and pleasure—work, child rearing, looking after someone other than oneself, travel and favorite activities— are things of the past. Family ties, though, remain important; often more so as other connections diminish and children try to fill in the gaps. For those who are blessed with mutual love and affection their life has meaning.

My mother takes a "Senior Citizens" bus each week to the supermarket. Among this small group of women the talk is almost entirely about children, grandchildren and their visits. What counts for these women is not the size of their children's salaries or the prestige of their position, but how much attention they pay to their parents. The one woman who rarely sees her daughter receives much sympathy. In general, most parents derive much pleasure from the gestures that show they are remembered and loved. Their wellbeing flourishes with the sense that they have done a good job in raising their children.

All of us feel depressed at times and have developed our own ways of coping. We get busy, take a walk, or visit a friend. Unfortunately, in advanced old age many of the habitual ways of dealing with low moods are no longer available. You may feel that life will always be desolate and empty. In your memories, the world of your young years was brighter and more vital; and it seems that life will never be as good again. But that does not mean that life will never be good again. There may be much to grieve but there will also be much to enjoy and appreciate. It seems to be a human characteristic that we always want more—more time, more love, more travel—or, if we cannot have more, let us be allowed to keep what we have. When I heard that my ailing father had died, my first reaction was that it could not be true. I had just booked a flight to visit him. It was not fair. It took me a few minutes to remember that I had had a wonderful visit with him a few weeks earlier, and that he, unlike me, was ready to let go.

It seems so obvious that we covet what we enjoy and want all good things to continue. And yet, this clinging brings unhappiness. Not only does it leave us pining for what cannot be, but it also robs us of the wonders that surround us. We all know people who are chronically unhappy because they cannot let go of their longing for what they no longer have. They become defined by their loss. We also know more people who, despite their pain, are able to move beyond themselves and show gratitude for what they have. As the losses of old age accumulate, it must be so easy to feel deprived and even unfairly treated. It is a wonder that so many maintain or rediscover their capacity for pleasure and interest in the world about them.

END OF LIFE

There comes a point when death exists not only as an inevitable part of a life, but also as a probability in the near future. Intellectually we know that all living things die and that, without decay, life could not exist. In my experience most old people do not fear death itself but rather the process. Our children also think about our dying but may be reluctant to raise their questions for fear of upsetting us—or themselves. If they do broach the subject, try to welcome it and respond to them honestly. If they are silent we need to take the initiative in raising those matters that need to be aired before we die. Our family should know what we want to happen when dying and death arrive.

If you would like some control over the end of your life you have some questions to ask, and answers to make. Should you become terminally ill and unable to make you own decisions, do you want to be kept alive at all costs, or be kept comfortable and allowed to die when your body is ready? Your wishes are much more likely to be carried out if you have talked to your family and doctor about what you want, and also have completed a Living Will and a Power of Attorney for Health Affairs.

Both legal documents come into play if two physicians declare that you are terminally ill and incapable of making your own medical decisions. In a Living Will you can specify what life-prolonging medical procedures you do, or do not want. In the Power of Attorney for Health Affairs you give someone of your choice the responsibility for making health decisions on your behalf.

On occasion, someone who is very sick or tired of living wishes to end his or her life before it happens naturally. If you feel that way, please try to explain your feelings to your children. Many suicides leave agonizing questions for the survivors. Your children may not see things as you do but it will help them later if you have talked.

LAST WORD

During the many decades you have known each other, you all, both parents and children, have had times of intimacy, of distance, and of something closer to neutrality when you were not as much on each others' minds. This last stage of life is often the most difficult one for parents and children. Most elderly people experience some pain and certainly physical discomfort, loss of their capacities and perhaps fear of what is to happen in their remaining time. For children, there are new demands —caregiving, worry and the knowledge of certain loss.

Advances in healthcare mean that in this country most of us live into very old age. The tragedy is that length of life does not necessarily correlate with quality of life. Too many people feel that their life has already lasted too long. One client told me that she wished she would fall asleep and not wake up, not because she had no pleasure in life but, as she put it, "I don't need any more. It is enough already."

Our society is not an easy one in which to be very old. The elderly have no recognized role, they often live in poverty and there are limited services to enable them to stay in their own homes. And for adult children who provide most of the help their parents need, that care often comes at a high cost. Since families may be separated by long distances, children try to oversee their parent's wellbeing via the telephone, trying to decide what constitutes a crisis and necessitates a visit. These responsibilities may be overwhelming especially to people who have children of their own, sick spouses or jobs that fill their days. Yet, the bonds of love and sense of responsibility are maintained and passed from parent to child to parent, from one generation to the next.

As we have learned, there are no rules about how people show concern for each other—only guidelines. When children perceive their parents failing and struggling to manage they have to tread a fine line between ensuring that their parents are as safe and comfortable as possible, and, at the same time help them to retain some sense that they are in charge. This is a difficult task at the best of times, and more so because each parent, each child and each situation is different. There is usually no right or wrong solution to any such dilemma, just a lesser of two evils. Moreover, the various parties rarely agree. Children are often concerned about practical problems and answers, whereas parents are happier with what is familiar and comfortable. Useful though practical help is, emotional sensitivity and understanding are equally important. For elderly people it may be that falling at home and not being discovered for 24 hours is a risk worth taking, and certainly preferable to living in assisted living, even if it is supposedly safer. A valuable guideline is for family members to talk to each other, covering all aspects of a problem and attempting to understand each other's point of view.

Why do children usually make considerable efforts on behalf of their parents? It may seem a strange question but it may be helpful. You will all generate you own personal list of answers. In caring for your parents you may be motivated primarily by love, by duty, by gratitude. You may be following the teachings of your religion, You may believe that everyone deserves to live out their lives as fully and comfortably as possible. When your parent dies you may want to believe that you did the best that you could. You are probably influenced by many of these considerations and others not mentioned.

Your personal list will reveal your own values and reasons for living. When you feel discouraged and bogged down with chores you will find that how you meet your responsibilities will be part of what gives your life meaning. Apparently menial tasks then assume more significance in the context of your wider purpose.

As parents, you too do your best to weather this last stage with grace. Though often hampered by pain and infirmity, you probably strive to be as uncomplaining as possible, to maintain your dignity and self-sufficiency and to nurture your love for your families.

What is our life all about? In the scale of things we exist on this earth for a very short time, but it is all we have. We seem to need to make sense of life and why we are here. I believe that most of us try to add to our world by being the best we can be. A few people are blessed with extraordinary creativity, intelligence and skills that bring benefits on a large scale, but that route is not for most of us. It is who we are and how we behave that make differences in our small world. We all know that a friendly word even, perhaps especially, from a stranger can make a difference to our mood, and that we are then more likely to smile at the next person we meet. Thus ripples spread and touch others.

Each of us can resolve to work at expanding the friendliness, good temper and tolerance in this world. In tiny but significant ways you will affect many people you do not even know; and will affect yourself too. Do not underestimate your impact. Above all, we pass light and goodwill to the members of our families. We have the best chance of influencing the people sitting next to us.

My hope is that you, parents and children, will find satisfaction in your relationship with each other in your last years together. While some of your difficulties will be unforeseen, or more painful than you could imagine, there will surely be warm, affectionate and amusing times. Do the best you can to convey your love, thanks and appreciation not only to each other but include the wider family. You belong to each other. Together you have built happy memories that connect you, and the upcoming generations will carry into the future.

Ruth Whybrow worked *for many years as a clinical social worker and geriatric specialist. In addition to her work as a psychotherapist in a regional mental health center and in private practice, she gave workshops, lectures, and led groups for the elderly, caregivers, and adult children.*

Her first book, Caring for Elderly Parents, *appeared in 1996. She was on the faculty of Smith College and Dartmouth Medical School. She now lives in Strafford, Vermont.*

Made in the USA
Charleston, SC
09 April 2011